Praise for 'Cracking the Code- The Fascinating Truth About Taxation In America' by Peter Eric Hendrickson:

"...a judicious and thoughtful work written by an American patriot deeply dedicated to the rule of law." "Skepticism and doubt will slowly be replaced with certainty and conviction as Hendrickson systematically walks his readers through the law and the tax code's maze of confusion."
Steve Thomas, The Mackinac Center for Public Policy, Midland, Michigan

"Thank you so much for your exquisitely documented and beautifully written "Cracking the Code"- "This book is a masterpiece of analysis, clarity and revelation." "This is brain candy for patriots!"
Christiane Sauter, Syracuse, New York

"Wow!!!! I've been studying this for 10 years and haven't gotten anything as clearly as you have put it in your book." "I cannot thank you enough..."
Joyce Cox, Afton, Wyoming

"All American Citizens who truly love their freedom and have a healthy skepticism of the federal government will add this book to their evidentiary foundation..." "...it's a beautiful thing you've done."
John Carpenter, Ann Arbor, Michigan

"Read the book in about 2 days. Very well done. I have been looking at the issue for about 5 years and you distill the info down in a way even the newbies can absorb. Well worth the asking price. I hope this really sells."
Ed Wahler, Fletcher, North Carolina

"EXCELLENT" "...very well written and accurate." "... I would highly recommend."
Dave Wissel, Lebanon, Ohio

"...a valuable tool, and a wealth of knowledge." "Thank you for all your research..."
Arleen Miller, Page, Arizona

"I found the book to be extremely beneficial even though I was fairly knowledgeable on the subject prior to reading the book." "It is definitely on my list of 'recommended reads. Thanks for a great book."
Phil Patana, St. Louis, Missouri

"...haven't been able to put it down. Great information and fabulously put together!"
Bart Goss, Stockbridge, Georgia

"This is a fabulous book I would highly recommend..."
Larry Golson, Montgomery, Alabama

After reading your book, I knew that you had found the answer that everyone

D1383235

"After receiving CtC I read it in a day or two (every spare minute I could get). It is the best book-- the best material-- I have read yet on the income tax issue." *"Thank you for your research and your great book..."*
Robin Kartchner, Pleasant Grove, Utah

"What a great book!"
John B. Gartner, West Chester, Pennsylvania

"...I just recently read your book 'Cracking the Code' and I love it. I have been studying the tax "problem" for about 6 years now and your book really crystallizes everything."
Karl Weatherly, Ketchum, Idaho

"Thank you so much for a well written book. It really gave me a lift."
Clyde H Shaulis, Jr., Erie, Michigan

"Thanks for the wonderful book."
Charley Harman, Black Diamond, Washington

"Great stuff! Thanks... ...for an excellent read and all the investigative historical research."
Ron Flick, Roland, Arkansas

"Excellent material..." *"You appear to have solved the puzzle, for which I am most grateful."*
James W. Sisk, Goodlettsville, Tennessee

"Excellent work. You have demystified the most misunderstood and misinterpreted elements of the so-called tax laws..." *"In particular, I enjoyed your philosophical and ideological commentaries on the nature of law, how it works, and why law must operate the way it was designed..."*
Grant Sterling, author of 'Forbidden Property: What You Don't Own Can Hurt You!'

"'Cracking the Code' has shocked and amazed me. Everything checks out... a more important book has never been written. Reading it is like taking the red pill in the movie 'The Matrix'. Thanks for showing me just how deep the rabbit hole goes."
Thomas H. deSabla, Silver Springs, Maryland

"Excellent..."
J. J. W., Akron, Ohio

"Received your book yesterday. Started reading at 11 PM, finished at 4 AM." *"I have 16 feet (literally 16' 4.5") of documents supporting just about everything in your book."* *"Your book should be required reading for every lawyer before being admitted to any Bar."* *"I hope you sell a million of them."*
John Green, Spring, Texas

"Thank you for your superb work..."
Chet West, Woodland Park, Colorado

To get a copy of 'Cracking the Code- The Fascinating Truth About Taxation In America' (ISBN 0974393606), visit www.losthorizons.com or your favorite bookstore.

Upholding the Law

And
Other Observations

by
Peter Eric Hendrickson

Printed in the United States of America
First printing March 2006
Second printing May 2009
ISBN 0-9743936-1-4

The cover art is a detail from 'Sunstorm' by the author;
oil on board, 30" x 40"

To order additional copies of this book, or others by Peter E. Hendrickson, visit
www.losthorizons.com or your favorite bookstore

This book is dedicated to my parents, Jack R. and Audra S. Hendrickson-- an extraordinary duo whose integrity, courage, grace and accomplishments are an inspiration to all who know them, and a source of deepest pride to their most fortunate children.

Contents

In 1787, upon emerging from the constitutional convention which formed the basis for our federal government, Ben Franklin was approached by a woman outside the hall.

"Mr. Franklin," she asked "What kind of government have you given us?"

"A Republic, madam," Franklin replied, "If you can keep it..."

Foreword
ഇ)ശ്രൂ

American energy independence is a hot topic of public policy debate these days. While discussing the subject with friends recently, I found myself entertaining the whimsical notion that we have been overlooking a vast reservoir of energy-- one capable of lighting all America. What is this huge store of untapped power? The furious spinning which is doubtless going on 24/7 in the grave of each and every one of the Founding Fathers during the last hundred years...

Actually, of course, the scarcity which the spirits of the Founders can address does not involve American "energy independence", but, rather, American "independence energy"-- that is, the will to stand up and demand, and, if necessary, defend, the individual liberty which is our birthright as human beings and our heritage as Americans. It is that "independence energy" that is the dominant theme of the collection you now hold in your hands.

It IS a collection, consisting of 27 individual essays written over the course of the past five or six years, and variable in both tone and specific subject matter. Nonetheless, each of these pieces shares with the others a definite commonality. Each focuses on a matter of public policy and/or law which is the object of a dedicated disinformation campaign conducted by an entrenched cadre of beneficiaries of its misunderstanding, the consequence of which, either immediately or eventually, is a significant diminishment of American liberty.

My consideration of some of these matters, such as federal gun control, taxes, and drug law enforcement, necessarily delves into the technicalities and nitty-gritty of statutes and case law. Others are treated in a more 'political' manner. Either way though, it is my hope that the reader will come away from each and every one of these studies armed with fog-cutting facts and perspectives.

Much more importantly, I hope to generate some "independence energy" by making two broad points of considerably different character. The first--the good news-- is that reason, and, where pertinent, the words and meaning of the law, continue to fully support the principles upon which America was founded.

The bad news is that as a people, Americans have so fallen out of the habit of upholding those principles that the good news is almost inconceivable to us. We have become so accustomed to the habit of submission to the appetites and ambitions of the corrupt and exploitative public institutions that have grown up among us that we now mistake those institutions for *uncontrollable*, when the sordid reality is that they are merely *uncontrolled*. We perceive reason and the law as having been hijacked by the enemies of liberty, when really they have just been abandoned by too many of their friends.

Reason and the law DO both stand on our side, but only when we stand too, animated with "independence energy". It is my hope that this collection will contribute somewhat to both the confidence and the conscience of which that energy is composed.

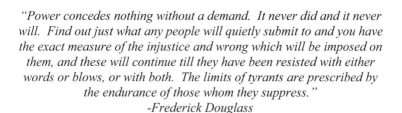

"Power concedes nothing without a demand. It never did and it never will. Find out just what any people will quietly submit to and you have the exact measure of the injustice and wrong which will be imposed on them, and these will continue till they have been resisted with either words or blows, or with both. The limits of tyrants are prescribed by the endurance of those whom they suppress."
-Frederick Douglass

This Is Not A Day For Empty Words
ഈ‍ＣＳ‍ऋऋ‍Ｑ‍ऋ

A couple of weeks ago, I sent out an email entitled 'Talk Is Cheap', in which I scornfully observed that while complaints about the overgrown, arrogant federal government are as common as scoundrels in politics, precious few Americans actually get up and take action. Today, as the latest strident diatribe against the "rogue Supreme Court" to cross my desk fades into the din of the hundred identical vaporous fulminations that preceded it, I find myself tempted to disregard my own words, descend to the same level of pointlessness as most of these screeds, and just bitch. Not at the recent Supreme Court majorities, though, however much that collection of knaves and villains may deserve it. No, my ire would be directed at the pundits and editorialists and public policy analysts who are filling the ether with clever, finely-crafted complaints and gripings-- each of which ends in a call to do... nothing.

This crowd of noise-makers, taken as a whole, constitute the safety-valve of the status quo. They start out echoing their reader's or listener's proper outrage, discuss the issue cleverly or amusingly... and end with an exhortation to write to Congress-- at best.

In many cases, the ending is even more pointless than that (something difficult to imagine, I know, when "writing to Congress" means urging a specialist in the compromising of principles, who is at the top of the beneficiaries-of-the-central-state heap, to take an uncompromising stand on principle, in order to diminish the power of the central state...). In many cases, these thundering, or delicately surgical, exercises of high dudgeon end in no more than a wry and clever witticism, which, even more than the ridiculous encouragements to "work within the system", express the real message of either variety: "Nothing can be done."

Needless to say, many-- if not most-- of those equipped with a pulpit capable of bringing their comments to the attention of a meaningful number of others are not at all interested in "anything being done". They themselves, self-evidently, are beneficiaries of the status quo. "Something being done" would, in one way or another, mean "something being done" *to them*.

This portion of the punditry tends to consist of those in the "write your congressman" category. They are among those who-- as libertarian commentator Harry Browne has put it-- play Lucy to the Charlie Browns of the world, endlessly promising that she won't pull the football away if he'll just trust her one more time.

They don't want to say outright that nothing can (or will) be done, for fear of encouraging their readers to look 'outside the box' for solutions. The enervation of public anger accomplished by this type of pundit is deliberate, and venal-- they want to divert the worried passengers from marching on the bridge by talking them into joining the "Issues To Be Brought To The Captain's Attention" draft revision committee, instead.

The rest are voices of despair and surrender, however much their expressions may be spiced with acid sarcasms. When they suggest that nothing can be done, these commentators don't mean "nothing *should* be done", like the others. Their message really is that "nothing <u>can</u> be done". Any critique of current affairs which is unaccompanied by a call for action in response unmistakably, if subtly, communicates that the situation is irremediably broken, and efforts to the contrary will be unavailing.

Many of the pundits in this latter category don't really care about the message at all, of course. They are merely exploiting public interest in the outrage of the day. They make a living putting the general dissatisfaction into clever words, by means of which their customers can vicariously vent, and then-- the situation having been duly taken cognizance of and found to be hopeless-- move on, with a sense that their civic duty has been fulfilled. A few of these passive observers DO care about the message; they are simply suckers for the "You can't fight City Hall" gimmick that has left corrupt city halls free to carry on unmolested for as long as humans have been out of the caves.

Right now both varieties of "nothing can be done" commentators are holding forth with gusto, voraciously feeding on the recent, merely corrupt, Kelo decision in which a majority on the U.S. Supreme Court defied the perfectly clear words of the people; and the corrupt and idiotic 'Ten Commandments' decision of a few days later. The fulminations against these outrages-de-jour have supplanted those directed at the Raich decision of a few weeks ago, and any still lingering in the air related to the court's upholding of the McCain-Feingold outrage last year (or any similar offenses in between). As in these earlier cases, and those others of the same sort issuing forth for lo, these many decades now, much ink will be spilled over last month's judicial defiance of the law of the land, but, as usual, little of it indeed will be devoted to declaring, "ENOUGH IS ENOUGH!"

No one blessed with a widely heard public voice will say, *"Hey. We can read. We know what the law says, even if the government and its court don't want to admit it."*
None will echo Andrew Jackson, who, in response to a Supreme Court ruling that he found wanting, famously declared, *"John Marshall has made his ruling-- now let* [us see] *him enforce it."*

No 'mainstream' pundit will, narrow-eyed and angry, urge Californians-- and citizens of the eight other sovereign states that have legalized certain uses of marijuana-- to carry on, and challenge the ludicrous and lawless ruling in the Raich case again-- and again, and again, and again, if necessary. (Nor will any call upon the California state police to interpose themselves between a Californian and her federal persecutors, although such was not an uncommon practice in this country's youth, when our appreciation of the blessings of liberty were less befuddled.)

Similarly, no talking-head, or writer with a national pulpit, will make a cause of seeing that the responsible city officials in New London, Connecticut are hounded from office, charged with corruption, and punished to the fullest extent of the law. After all, in giving the homes of Susette Kelo and several of her neighbors to another private interest, these officials have, for all practical purposes, accepted a bribe. An increase in tax money which city officials will spend shoring up the support of voters-- secured through an exercise of governmental power-- is nothing less. Nonetheless, these thieves will likely go unpunished, despite another good example offered by our ancestors: When the colonial government of Massachusetts undertook to effectuate a minor, but illegal, tax during the revolutionary period, the citizenry promptly burned an effigy of the proposed administrator of the tax, trashed the building in which he was to work, and drove the lieutenant-governor and his family from their home-- which was then demolished.

Well, each must be his or her own judge of how important it is that those to whom we have entrusted a monopoly on the initiation of force follow the rules we have laid down for them. I can't make anyone else value the preservation of their liberty as much as I do; and I can't force those who say "nothing can be done" to recognize that the only time something really can't be done is when everyone has decided to do nothing.

What I CAN do-- on, as it happens, this 229th anniversary of the signing of the Declaration of Independence-- is remind those few Americans that MY small voice reaches that July 4th is <u>not</u> the anniversary of our *achieving* independence. It is, rather, the anniversary of our deciding, and declaring to a candid world, that we will have it no other way. It is the anniversary of our resolution to <u>act</u> to secure our rights; and to never again leave, in the hands of any government, the determination of its own limits-- come what may.

<u>Read</u> the law. Raise <u>your</u> voice. <u>Act</u>. And keep in mind that the fireworks with which we mark this anniversary are not symbolic of a ticker-tape parade. They represent the bombs and bullets, and the din and clamor, of the long, bloody struggle of which Independence Day was but the beginning. We do not use them in celebration, but to remind ourselves-- year in and year out-- that liberty commands a dear price which true Americans must stand ever-ready to pay.

Tariff Time
ഇൗൽൟൟ

I've decided to empanel a commission to explore imposing tariffs and quotas on foreign executives doing the same kind of work as me. It's been a bit tough making ends meet lately, and I figure if I can have, say, 40% tacked on to the cost of the work product of all of these competitors, it'll be pretty easy to command some more green for old *numero uno*.

I'll appoint a proper group. I'm thinking of my bartender... somebody from the company holding my mortgage... that Teamster down the street... maybe the wife (nobody knows better than her how critical this is). I'm really not particular, as long as there isn't anybody that trades for any of that foreign talent (or mine). Wouldn't want to compromise the panel's objectivity!

If my commission determines that without the help I'll have to lay off my daughter's piano teacher, or miss a payment on a loan, or go into another line of work, they'll make the recommendation to President Bush that he levy a special tax on all that foreign competition until... well, indefinitely I guess, or until they're all out of business. Otherwise, we'll be right back in this crisis situation when the tax expires, and we'll have to do the whole thing all over again. Pretty inefficient, I think we'd all agree.

Now, I know I'll get some grief from the "free marketeers" out there, but they just don't understand (or won't admit) that a little protectionism like this is a small price to pay for keeping my skills (*local skills,* let's remember) well-honed. Otherwise, in a time of future need, it might take me days, if not weeks, to ramp back up to peak performance. Besides, the only reason the whole problem exists is that these other guys out there are *dumping* themselves on the market, working like slaves and overproducing every week. *They're probably all meth junkies.*

However, I'm not too worried about any political wrangling over this. I can surely count on the backing of every pol beholden, or wanting to be, to union support, and I've got a feeling that Bush will be amenable. He's gone for it before, and hey, what's sauce for the goose is sauce for the gander, right? The only people that'll get screwed by this are people who trade for my kind of work (or their customers), and as far as I can tell *they haven't got a lobby, or even a clue!* They won't know what hit 'em until they get the bill.

In the long run, my plan is good for America. It helps ensure that the wife and I will be less dependent on Social Security and similar publicly-funded goodies when we retire (or now, for that matter), and gives us more discretionary receipts in the meantime, *which go right into the domestic economy!* That means more money for the local shopkeepers and tradesmen, who themselves will spend a bit more freely as a result. Pretty soon we'll *all* be rich!

I think I'll start spreading some of this windfall right away on credit, without waiting for the President to act. It's practically a civic responsibility! Besides, in this business it doesn't hurt to be really hurtin', and, if I'm reading the signs right, the more economically tone-deaf you are while getting that way, the better. I've got a pretty good handle on that now: I've been studying the California state government, Amtrak, Big Steel and the domestic sugar cartel-- true giants in the industry.

That reminds me. Item #1 on that spending spree list has to be a couple of nice, fat donations to my friends in Washington. After all, they can't help you if they don't know you're out there.

But if they DO know you're out there, it's a whole different story. In that case, brother, *you can help yourself!*

The Mouse That's Roaring

(With apologies to Leonard Wibberley)

Although one might easily wish that it had been taken on behalf of a more comely issue, the stand on principle taken by many libraries across the country in the wake of the Supreme Court's recent opinion on the 'Children's Internet Protection Act' (CIPA) should be appreciated by all. Faced with the act's provisions for the withholding of federal funds from libraries that refuse to install internet filters restricting access to pornographic content, these local community organs have manfully told the feds to peddle their diktats elsewhere. In response, the feds have... done nothing. There is a valuable lesson to be gleaned from this apparent David-and-Goliath confrontation.

First, though, don't misunderstand. I am not cheering subsidized-- or simply facilitated-- access to either pornography or the internet. In fact, those aspects of this topic simply make clear to me that I am not capable of identifying a modern library's mission. In the past, I understood that mission to be making available as a community resource a collection of general interest literature and research materials too bulky, expensive, or occasional-in-utility to be reasonably acquired and maintained by individual citizens. The provision of smut would seem to me to be outside this scope. Even leaving aside the 'general interest' thing, from what I have seen, smut is cheap, compact, and insufficiently nuanced to require a great deal of variety for the full enjoyment of its "benefits". As for internet access, now that decent computers and internet services cost less than the televisions and cable services delivering passive-access garbage into most homes far too many hours a day, what is really being provided by the libraries in this regard is nothing more or less than a subsidy of the bad choice to have the one in the home in lieu of the other.

What I *am* cheering is the peek behind the curtain at the extreme limitation of federal authority made possible by the libraries' challenge of the CIPA in court and their subsequent reaction to the results of that challenge. Both elements of this little tempest-in-a-teapot combine to reveal an important truth that is usually more difficult to perceive.

First, in challenging the CIPA, the libraries obliged the Supreme Court to point out authoritatively that the act is Constitutionally sound without consideration of its dramatically limited application to recipients of federal grants. The act, after all, has nothing to do with content creation or distribution. It is designed to have no meaningful impact on adult access to even disfavored speech or information. Its only effect is upon access to such material for minors, restrictions on which have never suffered even a moment of peril in an American courtroom.

Consequently, as long as the federal government remained within its jurisdictional limits in crafting the act, it was good solid law, a fact which was known to its drafters. They had had two previous attempts wordily shot down by the court within the last decade (the 'Child Online Pornography Act' and the 'Communications Decency Act'), and were therefore working off a blueprint.

Reacting to the court's ruling, the libraries offer us the second part of the picture. Across the country these targets of the act are telling the federal government to keep its money (which for the most part was insignificant in amount) and are continuing with business as usual. That this is happening is a surprise to no one, including Congress-- libraries have made their intentions in this regard perfectly clear over recent years.

Considered together, these two aspects of the Child Internet Protection Act-- the lawfulness of the federal government's requirement that those within its jurisdictional reach deploy internet filters; and the guaranteed futility of that requirement when its application is limited to those receiving federal grants-- invoke a couple of questions. The answer comprises the unusually clear glimpse of the truth with which we are graced by our bevy of bellicose librarians.

The questions are these: Why did Congress construct this safe-as-houses act around the toothless federal funding connection? Indeed, why did Congress not simply equip the act with general application, and make it a federal crime to defy its protocol, thereby not only eliminating the opt-out being exercised by the libraries, but imposing its requirements upon every internet café, bookstore, and other venue at which equally hazardous internet access is made available?

The inescapable answer is simple: Because it can't, of course. The federal government *has no jurisdiction* in any union-state library, internet café, bookstore, etc. Not because it is prohibited by something in the Constitution, such as a First Amendment conflict, or the like; but because it has never been granted such jurisdiction.

*****

The whole concept of limitations to federal jurisdiction seems alien to many people. Playing along when the big kid on the block claims to be King of America has become so habitual that such people have forgotten that it's just play. Nonetheless, the truth is still honored in the mechanics of legislation, and, for the most part, in the courts. Every act of Congress contains either explicit or implicit acknowledgement of its limited scope of authority, and when judicial attention is properly drawn to those limits, even extreme legislative efforts to confuse or conceal the difference between what-is-desired and what-is-permitted fails.

The federal government is provided with general legislative authority only over its territories and possessions (among which are included areas ceded to that government by explicit union-state action). As was declared by counsel for the United States before the Supreme Court in United States v. Bevans, 16 U.S. 336 (1818):

> *"The exclusive jurisdiction which the United States have in forts and dock-yards ceded to them, is derived from the express assent of the states by whom the cessions are made. It could be derived in no other manner; because without it, the authority of the state would be supreme and exclusive therein,"*

with the court, in its ruling agreeing:

> *"What, then, is the extent of jurisdiction which a state possesses? We answer, without hesitation, the jurisdiction of a state is co-extensive with its territory;"*

In New Orleans v. United States, 35 U.S. (10 Pet.) 662, 737 (1836), the court reiterates this principle:

> *"Special provision is made in the Constitution for the cession of jurisdiction from the States over places where the federal government shall establish forts or other*

military works. And it is only in these places, or in the territories of the United States, where it can exercise a general jurisdiction. "

In 1956, the Eisenhower administration commissioned the Interdepartmental Committee for the Study of Jurisdiction Over Federal Areas within the States. The pertinent portion of its report points out that,

> *"It scarcely needs to be said that unless there has been a transfer of jurisdiction (1) pursuant to clause 17 by a Federal acquisition of land with State consent, or (2) by cession from the State to the Federal government, or unless the Federal Government has reserved jurisdiction upon the admission of the State, the Federal Government possess no legislative jurisdiction over any area within a State, such jurisdiction being for exercise entirely by the States, subject to non-interference by the State with Federal functions, and subject to the free exercise by the Federal Government of rights with respect to the use, protection, and disposition of its property".*

In addition, the federal government has administrative jurisdiction over its own organs and instrumentalities, and the authority to condition receipt of federally-dispensed funds pretty much as it wishes, as long as it is not egregiously discriminatory. It is also granted authority to regulate 'commerce among the states', which is Constitutionally meant as interactions between union-state governments-- a meaning which had suffered some misunderstanding during the middle part of the 20th century. Imaginative demagoguery during that period had briefly succeeded in floating the notion that 'commerce among the states' should be construed as meaning economic activity across state lines, or, in a still greater flight of fancy, as activity in one state which might theoretically affect economic activity in another state. But even laws written with the intention of exploiting this short-lived popular extravagance contain properly limiting language-- the opportunistic legislators relied upon the courts to overlook the limits, or for those opposed to the extra-legal ambitions of such acts to be unable to identify or articulate those limits.

The judiciary was indeed somewhat cooperative in these endeavors for a period of time; however, it is no longer so. Recent Supreme Court rulings striking down gun control, arson and domestic violence laws which sought to claim authority under these misconstructions serve to demonstrate this fact. Frankly, though, what has enabled legislative overreach has more commonly been poor performance in the ranks of those victimized by congressional excesses. As I noted above, while few federal enactments are as straightforward in acknowledging the government's jurisdictional limits as, for instance, the following anti-discrimination act:

> *Title 18 USC Sec. 244. - Discrimination against person wearing uniform of armed forces*
>
>> *Whoever, being a proprietor, manager, or employee of a theater or other public place of entertainment or amusement in the District of Columbia, or in any Territory, or Possession of the United States, causes any person wearing the uniform of any of the armed forces of the United States to be discriminated against because of that uniform, shall be fined under this title,*

even the most egregiously un-straightforward legislation nonetheless typically contains direct language confining it to its proper place. Where this is not the case, laws will at least lack any language which legally attempts a claim to the contrary, and are therefore, under fundamental doctrine, equally confined. As the Supreme Court has put it:

*"'All legislation is prima facie territorial.' Ex parte Blain,
L. R. 12 Ch. Div. 522, 528; State v. Carter, 27 N. J. L.
499; People v. Merrill, 2 Park. Crim. Rep. 590, 596.
Words having universal scope, such as 'every contract in
restraint of trade,' 'every person who shall monopolize,'
etc., will be taken, as a matter of course, to mean only
everyone subject to such legislation, not all that the
legislator subsequently may be able to catch."*
American Banana Co. v. United Fruit Co., 213 U.S. 347
(1909)

Look at a simple example of the 'hidden language'
approach, in the federal law purporting to require FDA approval
of new drugs, at Title 21 USC, Section 355. Rather than
acknowledging its limitations openly, the act deploys definitions
which incorporate such an acknowledgement while concealing
the fact from immediate view. This method allows the
legislators to wave what appears to be a robust exercise of
authority in the public interest before voters, and leaves the
inconvenient limitations to be revealed only later in obscure
courtroom contests.

Sec. 355. - New drugs
(a) Necessity of effective approval of application
*No person shall introduce or deliver for
introduction into interstate commerce any new
drug, unless an approval of an application filed
pursuant to subsection (b) or (j) of this section is
effective with respect to such drug.*

Sec. 321. - Definitions; generally
(b) The term "interstate commerce" means
*(1) commerce between any State or Territory
and any place outside thereof, and*

> *(2) commerce within the District of Columbia or within any other Territory not organized with a legislative body.*

Clearly, any drug maker that wished could set up shop in California, for instance, and sell to its heart's content within the 5th largest economy in the world without sending so much as a birthday card to the FDA. (Indeed, one has to wonder why the various state governments are not luring drug manufacturers to spin off units into their individual jurisdictions, so that the next innovation can be marketed to each state's citizens at far lower prices than is possible under the FDA regimen). But wait, there's more. Actually, the limitations on federal authority in this, and any similar case, is even more circumscribed than is apparent in the hidden, limiting language. As the Supreme Court points out in Eisner v. Macomber, 252 U.S. 189 (1920):

> *"...it becomes essential to distinguish between what is, and what is not 'income'...Congress may not, by any definition it may adopt, conclude the matter, since it cannot by legislation alter the Constitution, from which alone it derives its power to legislate, and within whose limitations alone, that power can be lawfully exercised."*

Under this common-sense doctrine, Congress lacks the authority to define or determine the extent of jurisdiction conveyed under Constitutional grants of authority. In the gun control case mentioned earlier, United States v. Lopez 514 U.S. 546 (1995), the court, in striking down the legislation, makes clear that the same principle expressly applies to the meaning of the term "commerce":

> *"Similarly, under the Government's "national productivity" reasoning, Congress could regulate any activity that it found was related to the economic productivity of individual citizens: family law (including marriage, divorce, and child custody), for example.*

Under the theories that the Government presents in support of 922(q) [the law in question], *it is difficult to perceive any limitation on federal power, even in areas such as criminal law enforcement or education where States historically have been sovereign. Thus, if we were to accept the Government's arguments, we are hard-pressed to posit any activity by an individual that Congress is without power to regulate."*

The court explicitly rejects the most expansive misconstructions of the recent past, citing John Marshall's ancient delineation of the meaning and limitations of the commerce clause in Gibbons v. Ogden, 9 Wheat 1, (1824):

"It is not intended to say that these words comprehend that [type of] commerce, which is completely internal, which is carried on between man and man in a State, or between different parts of the same State, and which does not extend to or affect other States. Such a power would be inconvenient, and is certainly unnecessary."

...

"Comprehensive as the word `among' is, it may very properly be restricted to that commerce which concerns more States than one. . . . The enumeration presupposes something not enumerated; and that something, if we regard the language or the subject of the sentence, must be the exclusively internal commerce of a State."

Five years after Lopez, in the 'Morrison' domestic violence case, the court reiterates this doctrine while nullifying another overreach by Congress:

"Congress found that gender-motivated violence affects interstate commerce "by deterring potential victims from traveling interstate, from engaging in employment in interstate business, and from transacting with

*business, and in places involved in interstate
commerce;...* " *Given these findings and petitioner's
arguments, the concern that we expressed in Lopez that
Congress might use the Commerce Clause to completely
obliterate the Constitution's distinction between national
and local authority seems well founded"* United States
v. Morrison, 99-5 (2000)

At the very least, with these recent rulings the court is
saying that regardless of what Congress might declare its
intended meaning of "commerce" to be, the term cannot be
extended to convey jurisdiction except insofar as, and during
the time that, the object of legislative attention crosses state
lines. The court's growing impatience with congressional
ambitions in this regard is unsurprising. Look at another recent
law, even more optimistic in the sort of overreach which the
court is no longer prepared to tolerate: The Clean Water Act.

The 'Clean Water Act' provides, among other things, for
supervision of matters affecting "navigable waters". "Navigable
waters" are defined within the act to mean "waters of the
United States including the territorial seas". This language is
commonly cited as representing a claim of authority under the
act to dictate behavior by anyone with respect to anything wet
that is more substantial than a temporary puddle left on the
sidewalk after a thunderstorm.

When we look at the regulations under which this
authority is implemented, we find, as expected, what purports
to be the requisite limiting language. However, that language
dramatically fails the tests of both common sense and the
increasingly bright line being laid down by the court in regard to
the meaning of "commerce":

33 CFR §328.3 Definitions.
*For the purpose of this regulation these terms are
defined as follows:*
(a) The term "waters of the United States" means

(1) All waters which are currently used, or were used in the past, or may be susceptible to use in interstate or foreign commerce, including all waters which are subject to the ebb and flow of the tide;

(2) All interstate waters including interstate wetlands;

(3) All other waters such as intrastate lakes, rivers, streams (including intermittent streams), mudflats, sandflats, wetlands, sloughs, prairie potholes, wet meadows, playa takes, or natural ponds, the use, degradation or destruction of which could affect interstate or foreign commerce including any such waters:

(i) Which are or could be used by interstate or foreign travelers for recreational or other purposes; or

(ii) From which fish or shellfish are or could be taken and sold in interstate or foreign commerce; or

(iii) Which are used or could be used for industrial purpose by industries in interstate commerce;

(4) All impoundments of waters otherwise defined as waters of the United States under the definition;

(5) Tributaries of waters identified in paragraphs (a)(1)-(4) of this section;

(6) The territorial seas;

(7) Wetlands adjacent to waters (other than waters that are themselves wetlands) identified in paragraphs (a)(l)-(6) of this section. Waste treatment systems, including treatment ponds or lagoons designed to meet the requirements of CWA (other than cooling ponds as defined in 40 CFR 123.11(m) which also meet the criteria of this definition) are not waters of the United States.

(8) Waters of the United States do not include prior converted cropland. Notwithstanding the determination of an area's status as prior converted cropland by any other federal agency, for the purposes of the Clean

> *Water Act, the final authority regarding Clean Water Act jurisdiction remains with EPA.*

Little further comment or analysis than the mere recitation of these definitions themselves is necessary. They are self-evidently absurd, and self-evidently unlawful. The 'principle' informing them could as readily be deployed to place every square foot of land in America, and every thing else as well, under federal jurisdiction.

Nonetheless, lives have been ruined through the invocation of these ridiculous pretenses, because the victims, being so much in the habit of playing along when the big kid on the block claims to be King of America, didn't even think to read the law by which they were being railroaded. It must be imagined that the Supreme Court is longing for an appropriate litigant who has read, and will argue against, this abominable legislative fantasy before the kid has accumulated so much control during play that he really *is* king.

*****

Librarians, rightly or wrongly, are seldom thought of as forceful personalities. Indeed, they have long been stereotyped as quiet, shy, *mousy* ladies, at their most militant when raising a finger to lip and issuing a peremptory "Shhhh!". Today, it's a different finger entirely that is on display, and the "shhh!" directed at that big noisy kid in the Fantasy section is more of a, *"Put a sock in it!"* It may be overstating it to call their expression a roar, but they're not whispering either. The rest of us will do well to listen.

A Modest Proposal For A New Industrial Policy
ഇ൘ങ൞ൻ

As is typical at the start of a school year, the tax-funded education industry is rolling out another of its perennial whines for a funding hike, airing the hoary proposition that success in public schooling is available... but only if we all fork out a little more money. This despite the record of the last 70 years during which expenditures on that industry steadily increased while performance steadily declined.

For instance, we were taxed an average of $867 per pupil in 1930, with that figure rising to $6,043 in 1993 (both figures in 1992 dollars). Despite this phenomenal increase, during the same period test scores dropped. In 1967 verbal SAT averages were 466, and math averages were 492. By 1991, verbal scores were down to 422, and math had dropped to 474.

Current numbers appear higher, but this is the result of simple fraud-- prior to the 1995 cycle the test's scoring template was "re-centered", incorporating a 100 point drop in the average raw score into the scale and resulting in nominal scores above those of previous years. ACT results over the last decade have continued to reflect the trend of decline no longer acknowledged by the SAT. Along with the explosion of remedial courses in colleges across the country, this unadulterated measure reports clearly that nothing has changed regarding the shoddiness of the "education industry" product.

The picture painted by these U.S. Department of Education numbers is highlighted by some additional statistics from the same source: While in 1960 the average student to teacher ratio was 25.8 to 1, by 1995 it had dropped to 17.3 to 1; over that same period the percentage of teachers with master's degrees more than doubled (to more than half) and the median years of teacher experience increased from 11 to 15. Nonetheless, we continue to be told that we just haven't spent enough to allow the industry to achieve success.

Thankfully, every home-schooled kid in the country decisively puts the lie to such nonsense. Academically, these students, on average, far exceed their public-schooled peers-- despite relevant per-pupil expenditures that are a tiny fraction of what is spent on those institutionalized counterparts. As reported in Lawrence Rudner's 1999 analysis of the largest study of its kind to that point, involving 20,760 students:

> *"Almost 25% of home school students were enrolled one or more grades above their age-level peers in public and private schools.*
>
> *Home school student achievement test scores were exceptionally high. The median scores for every subtest at every grade (typically in the 70th to 80th percentile) were well above those of public and Catholic/Private school students.*
>
> *On average, home school students in grades 1 to 4 performed one grade level above their age-level public/private school peers on achievement tests.*
>
> *Students who had been home schooled their entire academic life had higher scholastic achievement test*

scores than students who had also attended other educational programs.

There were no meaningful differences in achievement by gender, whether the student was enrolled in a full-service curriculum, or whether a parent held a state issued teaching certificate."
(Rudner, L. M. (1999a). Scholastic achievement and demographic characteristics of home school students in 1998.)

Surveys of homeschooling families consistently report average per-student expenditures of well below $1000 per year. For that matter, even private-schooled children consistently, if far less dramatically, out-perform public-schooled kids for, typically, half the money. The lesson is that spending is irrelevant to success-- it is incentive that makes the difference.

It will be observed that the homeschooling expenditure figure mentioned above does not include the value of the 10 or so weekly educational hours each home-schooled student receives from the teaching parent. However, as the relevant issue is not what the education of any given child costs that child's parents but rather whether additional spending on public schools can produce similar results, that value is moot. It is, after all, associated with services which are by their nature unavailable as discrete market goods and are capable of exchange only from a parent to that parent's child, regardless of amounts spent. Furthermore, that value is not the product of any training, specialty or other quantifiable characteristic toward which such spending could be targeted.

Even boundless optimism denying that simple economic reality can't support a case for more spending on the public schools-- and, in arguing the point, helps reveal its futility. In light of the insignificant spending of homeschoolers on all other academically-related expenses, it is clear that nothing but the securing of much better quality teachers, or far more mediocre ones-- in an effort to replicate the quality and focus of the homeschooling parent-- could offer any hope of benefit from increased spending.

The former, of course, could only be a viable potential solution if the teachers we have now are no good (or are deliberately holding back on their performance in order to blackmail the community into paying them more by ruining its children's futures until such demands are met). Since we are assured by both the school administrators and the teachers that we are already getting the best available (no one lobbying for more money is accompanying his or her efforts with a standing offer to resign in order to make way for the better quality replacement secured by the sought after higher salary...)-- and that they are working their very hearts out-- expectations of success from this spending-more-to-get-better-quality approach will prove to be misplaced.

The latter would require that we finance one full-time teacher with benefits, administrative expenses, support personnel, bussing, etc. for no more than every couple of students-- while still failing to secure an educator even remotely as committed to the success of the endeavor as Mom or Dad. Clearly, we'd be better off simply to offer all parents of school-age children a pro-rated share-per-child of what would be spent on such a teacher's salary, in order to encourage more of them to attend to their children's education directly. That way we would maximize the benefits of that group's proven record of success-- while enjoying bus-free roads, to boot.

(Actually, those parents already taking responsibility for their own children's education would be more than content at simply being spared the school taxes taken from them, for which they receive no benefit whatsoever. I'm confident that most others, upon joining their ranks, would take the same view. More on this in a moment.)

What this leaves are the other public-education-industry expenses by which increased spending is sometimes justified, such as infrastructure, diversity counselors, "Gay, Lesbian,

Bisexual and Trans-Gendered safe rooms", armed guards, STD treatment centers, drug-rehab facilities, book-banning committees, etc. All of these are ancillary to the whole surrogate-teacher concept, of course. Given the futility and indefensibility of that core program, spending on such 'perks' at any level can be seen as nothing more or less than throwing good money after bad.

Our hundred-year-old national experiment with government schools has been degenerating into fiscal irresponsibility and personal tragedy for its young victims for decades now. It is way past time to face the facts on this score, and acknowledge that the education of children is a responsibility properly attendant upon parenthood. Happily, as in so many other areas, giving propriety its due naturally and harmoniously delivers the best possible results.

We will never be entirely without a public education industry, of course-- there will always be orphans, and the children of addicts and the irremediably self-absorbed, for whom the provision of such welfare will be the unavoidable obligation of a charitable society. But we can and should recognize that this option is the worst of all possible worlds from an educational standpoint-- delivering the poorest results for the most money.

The best option, homeschooling, may not be for everyone (although learning the truth about the 'income' tax would negate one of the chief obstacles for many-- the loss of one parent's earnings). But as a society, we should be encouraging it as broadly as possible. Recourse to the next best alternative, private schools, should also be supported. In both cases, the single most significant public policy change that could effect such support and encouragement would be the crediting of all taxes earmarked for their own children's education to parents not using the public system.

Simple fairness demands such a policy, and even though for some this would mean an insignificant reduction in taxes, it would be enough to induce many-- who otherwise feel that since they're being made to pay for the public system anyway, they may as well use it-- to take direct charge of their children's education, or at least move to the private school option. Each one of those not currently paying their children's entire public-school ticket through their own taxes who makes that choice would leave more money per student in that system; those paying more than is spent on their kids would continue to pay the excess, with the same beneficial result.

Here's an example: Presume that per-student government spending is $10,000. When a family with one child of school age which currently pays $5,000 in school taxes keeps that child out of the public schools, its tax bill goes down by the $5,000. The $5,000 balance however, which has been being subsidized by others all along, stays with the public school system, resulting in a net gain of that amount for the system. On the other hand, if that family is currently paying $12,000 in school taxes, they keep the $10,000 when they pull their child out of public schooling, but continue to pay the other $2,000-- again resulting in a net gain for the public school system. Those who had been paying exactly what is spent on their own children would have no effect on the existing system at all.

On balance then, public schooling would have more money per student, and society as a whole would gain better-educated citizens. Ultimately (and quickly) the tax burden on those subsidizing other people's kids would go down as the public education industry found itself with more and more money for fewer and fewer students, delivering even more benefits more broadly. It's a win-win solution.

Interestingly, one of the groups that would enjoy the greatest net benefit from this policy would be public school teachers who, on average, have half again as many of their own children in private schools as does the general population of parents, according to the U.S. census. I'm sure I can count on their enthusiastic support for my plan...

Hold That Bus!

ℰꙴℬꙴℛ

As the primary season of another election year
descends upon the nation, accompanied by the usual plagues of
campaign signs and junk mail, voters in many urbanized areas
are also facing the perennial eruption of tax-funded
boondoggles marring their ballots. These proposals are all
touted as either the magic charm that will reverse the decline of
the central mega-city, such as casinos or a new sports arena, or
the provision of a desperately needed personal service that
somehow the market is disinclined or unable to address, such as
mass transit or the maintenance of cultural centers.

Southeastern Michigan, where my family makes its
home, is one such area currently bedeviled by boosters of a
mass-transit plan. Interestingly, the notion, which requires
state legislative action in order to proceed, is complicated at
that level by efforts to include language in the enabling
legislation allowing any given county to opt out of the plan-- an
accurate reflection of the sensible disinterest that this plan
enjoys among those who would pay for it.

Indeed, the results of a recent University of Michigan
survey on attitudes towards mass transit in southeastern

Michigan, published on March 20th, 2002, reveal that most of the area's residents realize what never-say-die boosters of tax funded transportation schemes simply won't face-- that the central mega-city, which is the only organizational form for which mass transit truly makes sense, is a thing of the past,... and good riddance. While at one time the economic and technological limits on personal transportation made giant, dense-packed concrete jungles infested with corrupt political machines, crime, and limited horizons virtually unavoidable, those limits have been overcome and the cities are being abandoned as fast as possible. The University found that 68% of respondents to its poll had no interest in funding any mass transit, that 70% had no interest in living in a community designed around a mass transit system, and indeed, only 5% of area residents ever made any use of the mass transit options (regional bus system; People Mover elevated rail) already in place.

All over the United States cities are shrinking and suburban and rural areas are growing as people escape the pathologies of urban living. According to U.S. government figures, while in 1960 the number of people living in cities and suburbs was the same, as of 2 years ago there were 1.65 times as many suburbanites as city dwellers. And this trend cuts across demographic lines as well; by the year 2000 fully 39% of all black households in the United States were suburban.

Despite this reality, those clinging to power-bases in existing central cities shill for a constant stream of silver bullet solutions that will 'turn the city around', as if spending enough of other people's money will repeal the laws of nature. Actually, the laws under assault are the laws of economics, which the political hack class learned long ago can be, if not repealed, at least usefully distorted. They know that once enough money has been spent on some dumb project, or series of projects, it becomes increasingly easy to talk voters out of walking away from the "investment".

Furthermore, as the trough begins to fill a cadre of very interested beneficiaries willing and able to chunk out campaign money and become politically active in defense of that pork springs up like toadstools in a swamp after the rain. The mass-transit scheme being pushed for metro Detroit, involving a radical upgrading and expansion of the existing unused bus system and the eventual addition of various light rail routes into the central city, is no exception. It's a dumb idea by which a tiny market will be poorly served, and which will cost a fortune. Just the bus system upgrade alone is estimated (by its supporters) to soak up 2 billion "investment" dollars over the next 25 years ($80 million per year), in addition to a perpetual $200 million each and every year in operating expenses. Then light rail gets piled on top.

The need for a $200 million annual operating subsidy reveals the truth about the market for the bus system-- there isn't one. The fact that terminals built for mass-transit light rail schemes are typically equipped with every parking space the planners can scrape up reveals the truth about the light rail concept: people *drive* to the mass-transit terminals, and then only if they can't drive to where they really want to go. For most people and in most cases mass-transit will never be any more than a slow and inconvenient fallback should the road and parking infrastructure serving their desired destination become-- forgive me-- 'overtaxed'.

In fact, boosters of such schemes rely on the paucity and condition of parking options in the central cities to help make their publicly funded private cash cow attractive, or at least less smelly, without giving a moment's thought to simply spending a tenth as much money on adding safe, convenient parking downtown, which would completely satisfy the ever-diminishing demand for travel into that destination-- and with little, if any, ongoing public expense. The interests of those

traveling out of the city are ill-served by mass-transit as well--
because once you get out here in the suburbs, you'd better
have a car!

Of course, the plan is that such outbound riders will use
the bus system once they get into the suburbs. But if they're
coming out to work or shop, they can afford to pay for
transportation. If it's just sightseeing, I have a problem with
spending a combined $280 million a year plus the unknown
costs of the light rail system in order to subsidize tourism by 5%
or less of the area population. Frankly, the $280 million could
buy 28 million $10 cab rides each year. If there is a real need
for welfare in transportation, let's just hand out taxi vouchers.

Rather than spend time and resources on dinosaur
concepts like mass-transit, regional planners should focus on the
encouragement of telecommuting and the elimination of
licensure barriers to a brisk free market in taxi, jitney, and
microbus service-- transit options suited to the sprawling,
decentralized living arrangements that most tax-payers and
voters prefer. In addition to being incomparably more flexible in
performance, vastly more resource-efficient and infinitely more
adaptable to actual demand than any mass transit option, such
market-based approaches enjoy the additional cachet of being
in tune with the times. Though I'm reluctant to flog even a
quiver out of the wildly over-exercised 9-11 horse, I can't resist
pointing out that, within the context of that particular crisis-of-
the-hour, the notion of spending money on packing large
numbers of citizens into buses or rail cars is almost ludicrously
counter-intuitive.

If all goes well, a time will come when our
grandchildren will take their kids on wide-eyed tours of the
empty canyons, abandoned buildings, and silent overgrown
miles of tiny, crowded residential plots that the cities will have
become, explaining with a forgivable touch of condescension

that this was the way people were forced to live before private, personal vehicles and effective telecommunications technology were fully developed. Then they'll all pile back into their car and drive home-- to the suburbs.

Regarding The Law And Its Virtues
ဆာ ౪8౦ ౧

A society transforms itself into a state through the adoption of law. By the use of law, what had been more-or-less spontaneous interactions of conflict are regularized and formalized. This more reliably secures to each participant the benefits of predictability and stability (and that of a superior defensive capacity against individuals or organizations which might seek to subjugate them). Law provides these benefits by replacing the vagaries of custom and tradition with demonstrably authorized, written, unambiguous and procedurally scrupulous rules governing the interactions of the participants, backed by the cooperative and coordinated actions of each such participant.

When performing its legitimate purpose, the law is a great blessing to all. When carelessness or ignorance permit its application to illegitimate purposes, the enormous power of a coordinated and cooperative society becomes a potent tool for the satisfaction of private interests and the abuse of political targets, as well as the imposition of tyranny. It is possible to measure the character of that which claims status as law by its conformity to three essential principles: 1. Legitimacy of authority; 2. Clarity of command; and 3. Conformity with established procedures of notice.

Though once the very pinnacle of respect for legitimate rule of law (and the most richly rewarded beneficiary thereof), the United States has fallen deeply from that high ground. An analysis of the essential principles of law will reveal how we have stumbled, and provide guidance as to how to once again find the right path.

But first, Sovereignty

Before discussing the characteristics of law, which is the product of a state, it is necessary to briefly comment on sovereigns, who are the precursors to the state. A sovereign is a free-standing, independent agent, whose right to exist and act are inherent by nature. While much weird and degenerate philosophy has been fabricated over the centuries alleging social contracts, mystical fatherlands, divine right and the like, ad nauseum, the simple and incontrovertible facts are:

- *No human being can assert a claim of authority by right over any other human being;*
- *All human agencies are merely subordinate constructs which can claim no authority beyond that of their creators; furthermore, such agencies can assert nothing for themselves, and assertions made on their behalf can have no demonstrable standing beyond that of the speaker or speakers-- who are just other human beings;*
- *No one can claim rights superior in quantity or quality to those of anyone else.*

Therefore, regardless of whether or not each of us really has a right to act freely, no one else has a right to interfere with our acting freely. So, we are all sovereign by default at least, if not by design. Our power-to-act is not dependent upon or answerable to any other person or any other person's creation.

States, on the other hand, are not sovereign, except as to other states. This will be discussed in more detail below. On to the law...

*****

1. Legitimacy of Authority

The starting point of any law is the authority of the legislators. A law can only issue from an agency to which those upon whom the law will act have delegated appropriate authority. Such authority can be broad or narrow, depending upon the wishes of the delegator, but is in all cases limited and explicit-- for the authority to withdraw, modify or define any delegation cannot itself be delegated. A delegation, after all, is an assignment, not a negotiation; furthermore, only that over which an individual has authority himself can be delegated to another.

"Authority" means *creatorship*, or, because the attributes of the created are as designed by the creator, *the rule of the created by the creator. (The root of the word is the Latin, "auctor", which means "creator". The principle which is addressed here doesn't rest on semantics, of course, but as is often the case, the etymology of the appropriate term can clear away cobwebs of confusion spun by its promiscuous misuse.)* Being possessed of authority over their own decisions, individuals can delegate the making of such decisions to an agent, and can agree to adopt such decisions as their own and act accordingly. The quality of self-directed independence (sovereignty) however, is not under human authority and therefore cannot be delegated to the state. Thus, the state can have no standing or interest on behalf of which its spokesmen may properly dispute, redefine, qualify or interpret the terms of the delegation. The state is not a party to the deal and is, insofar as its own nature is concerned, voiceless.

It is, after all, the delegation itself which creates the state. The creation cannot partake of the decision by which it is created; that is, the state cannot authorize its own authority. Not only is such a lifting-oneself-up-by-one's-own-bootstraps impossible temporally, it is also impossible legally, for it would create a dysfunctional and irresolvable tension between competing authorities. The creation would argue with the creator, from equal standing, as to what authority has been granted it-- the legal equivalent of two bodies occupying the same space at the same time.

Further, even if the metaphysical impediments could be overcome, such a delegation *could not* be accomplished, for it would constitute an unmistakable act against the delegator's own interests, be evidence of an unsoundness of mind, and therefore be void. Basic logic and legal principle establish that one cannot competently or effectively choose to divest oneself of the power to delegate, or to be the sole determinant of the meaning and extent of delegations made, or otherwise compromise one's sovereignty. Simple natural law precludes the possibility as well-- as Samuel Adams, the Father of the American Revolution, points out,

> *"If men, through fear, fraud, or mistake, should in terms renounce or give up any natural right, the eternal law of reason and the grand end of society would absolutely vacate such renunciation. The right to freedom being the gift of Almighty God, it is not in the power of man to alienate this gift and voluntarily become a slave."*

Nor, of course, can one individual be bound by delegative choices made by another. Any individual has only the capacity to delegate his own deliberative and decision-making powers, not those of his neighbor.

Although these points about the subordinate, voiceless nature of the state seem elementary upon examination, violations of the principle are now routine in America, in service to factions wishing to exercise illegitimate power for their own benefit at the expense of their neighbors. This is done through a corrupt and corrupting sophistry which twists legitimacy of authority and sovereignty into conveniences of the politically powerful.

The process can be perceived by consideration of any victimless "crime". Because the relevant behavior involves no conflict in regard to which the participants might have an interest in the benefits of law, no credible or proper basis for a relevant delegation authorizing state involvement can be alleged. Also, of course, no victim with standing from which to seek suppressive redress can be called upon. Factions which wish to nonetheless assert power over their neighbors in regard to the disapproved behavior must overcome these infirmities.

To do so, they posit a mysticism by which the aggregate mass of delegators, personified by the state, has, *prest-o change-o!*, acquired sovereignty-- and sovereignty of superior stature to that of any of its individual parts. This magical sovereign claims standing as an aggrieved party where no real one can make a complaint, so as to legitimize calling upon itself for remediation from the "offense". Godlike, this sovereign exists at all times and in all places, available to be offended against whenever and wherever any vile perpetrator acts, and, being relieved of the necessity of proving personal injury, it admits to no meaningful limit as to the behavior within its reach. Thus the state creates its own authority to act at will, by self-proxy-- where no authority to act by delegation exists. Which is to say, those in control of the state's power create-- all on their own-- new authority under which it will act, doing their will.

Partaking of the fiction of the magic sovereign is the philosophically complementary proposition that each and every person within the state's reach can be presumed, whether they acknowledge it or not, to have entered into an unwritten contract with it and owe it performance, which notion finds expression in the concepts of *duty to the state* and *offenses of omission*. Both are invoked heavily either directly or sub-textually in support of much improper behavior by the state.

Another pernicious consequence of this construct is the recent trend toward direct adoption of its principles by various factions, in a bizarre balkanization of the polity into a multitude of magic sovereigns. So-called "hate crimes", which amount to the criminalizing of behavior causing no demonstrable harm to any individual but offending the sensibilities of a sub-community of identity-- according to its spokespeople-- serve as examples.

Whether the conduct being targeted (or demanded) through these legal and philosophical contortions is good or bad is not at all the point-- the point is the ugliness of narrow political interests adopting the mantle of an imaginary authority backed by all the vast power delegated to the state, for any purpose whatever.

2. Clarity of Command

A second essential element of proper law is clarity. Just as the delegation of authority must be explicit, so too must the product of the legislators to whom such delegations have been made. Clearly, no benefits over the soft and fuzzy admonitions of custom and tradition are extended by law which is ambiguous or subjective, or prone to constant interpretation and re-interpretation. Indeed, the entire purpose of law-making is to inform those to whom it applies precisely what is expected of them by others and how those others will formally react to any given behavior.

Law which can only be applied with the assistance of interpretation is therefore improper and void-- such law not only provides no usable notice of its requirements to those for whose interests it is purportedly crafted, but becomes necessarily the law of the interpreter rather than that of the delegatees. While an argument in defense of such free-form law has been advanced, to the effect that those delegatees are merely delegating authority in their turn, this proposition fails. Such delegatees do not have, and cannot delegate, such authority. Their only authority is what has been delegated to them, and they cannot be given the power of self-direction.

This is not to say that a delegation could not include the command that under this or that circumstance, and regarding this or that particular, law-making authority will pass to this or that other organ of the state. A command of this sort could even refer to this complication with language such as, "When such and such is the case, the legislature shall delegate law-making authority to the executive (or the judiciary)", although it would be an example of poor construction. What is really being said, however (the awkward language notwithstanding), is that when the specified circumstances obtain, the delegators withdraw the delegation from the legislature and grant it to the executive (or whoever) instead.

This principle is so elementary and fundamental that it needs no elaborate analysis. The law must mean what it says, and say what it means, or there is no purpose to it whatsoever. We do not establish a legislature, and delegate authority thereto, in order to guess at the meaning of its products or learn of their requirements and nuances only once charged with their violation, and in jeopardy of life, liberty or property.

Notably absent from our delegation of authority to the state is any providing that in cases in which the legislature should produce incomprehensible or even simply ambiguous "law", authority transfers to the judiciary under which that branch can "interpret" and "clarify" such flawed enactments. Judges are charged with the responsibility for overseeing the fair and proper enforcement of what the law IS, not of what it SHOULD be, or what they imagine the legislature must have meant. That the judiciary is empowered to rule an enactment unconstitutional is not an exception to this truth; such a ruling is no more than a declaration that the enactment in question either fails to provide clarity of command; exceeds delegated authority; or violates the requirements of proper notice (which we shall examine shortly). No law is thus promulgated by those to whom such authority has not been delegated. Sophomoric late-night-dorm-room protestations to the contrary notwithstanding, to say what something *isn't* does not amount to saying what it *is*, (which principle applies equally to the saying of what the delegated authority-- itself, by the way, also capable of insufficient clarity-- isn't).

Furthermore, the law must be expressed such that each participant can understand its requirements and nuances for themselves. No member of a society can properly be subject to the risks of being on the losing end of a conflict of interest with an interpreter, or be obliged to trade with an industry of translators in order to have explained what has been done with their own delegation of authority! The principle of rational self-interest precludes the legitimacy of such legislation, as much as does that of primary authority. That proper law is thus necessarily limited in both its scope and its depth is a facet of an elegant dynamic favoring the minimalist state. There will, of course, always be some members of a society who cannot (or will not) comprehend some laws crafted by the associated state. Such persons cannot be viewed as having given their consent for those laws. They must be viewed as outside such laws. To the degree that such laws address transgressions against other members of society, non-consentors can be subject to their restraint-- the authority of self-defense thus exercised by those other members is unalienable and itself precedential to the state-- but cooperation with requirements-to-act (all versions of which amount to acts in support of the state), cannot properly be expected of them. No one can be legitimately enslaved to the interests of others, however untidy such a prohibition may seem. The practical application of this is that, once again, the state must remain small and simple.

Despite the obviousness of the principle of clarity of command, courtrooms across the United States are filled with defendants-- rich and poor alike-- being made to answer to a "law" which in many cases specifically excludes them from its ambit, but is deliberately written so as to encourage misunderstanding of this fact. Even more victims are held to account for requirements allegedly to be found among the incomprehensible hundreds of thousands of words of which many "laws", crafted to serve political rather than societal purposes, are made-- words which neither the judges, prosecutors, or defense attorneys could make even a credible pretense of having actually read.

3. Conformity to Established Procedures of Notice

The third pillar of legal propriety concerns the means by which the requirements of the law are made known to those on whom they will have effect. The legal cliché that, "Ignorance of the law is no excuse" can be true enough, but only where proper law prevails. Ignorance of a law passed in secret, or ambiguously crafted, is a complete and perfect excuse. No one can be held to account for a law the existence, meaning, or authority of which is kept from them, or is otherwise unavailable. Thus it is an essential principle that a consistent and effective means of notice be established and deployed.

As in all else regarding the law, ambiguity cannot be tolerated as to notice. A legitimate state will institute, and scrupulously abide by, explicit and well publicized rules for the construction, language, and dissemination of the law. (Indeed, no less than as regards clarity of meaning, a failure to do so must be viewed as an attempt to create a favored class within the greater host of participants, equipped with knowledge to be ransomed to their fellows.)

Laxness, even in the case of law related to the simplest and most common-sense behavior for which long and deeply established bodies of custom and tradition might exist, is unjustified and unacceptable. The necessity of rigid conformity to rules regarding form and notice is still more essential for statutes not enjoying such universal and instinctive embrace.

The very pinnacle of the importance of this principle attends statutes purporting to require positive action, as opposed to restraint. Such requirements are not natural to human interaction, and, unlike those imposing restraint, they involve no other interactive member whose competing interests an actor's behavior directly affects and who could therefore play a role in the notice process. (Restraints on purely private individual behavior are not under consideration here; they are all illegitimate.) The associated complications are undesirable, and are fertile ground for misunderstanding and the development of intricate-- and therefore error-prone-- case law. Thus, it bears repeating: requirements of positive action under the law must be most scrupulously clear in authority, construction and notice.

The importance of respect for this principle, particularly as regards the element of clarity, can be illustrated by a look at America today. The mechanisms of proper form and notice are diligently provided for in the American legal structure, including two key elements in the United States Code:

> *Title 1, Chapter 2, Section 101- Enacting Clause:*
> *"The enacting clause of all Acts of Congress shall be in the following form: "Be it enacted by the Senate and House of Representatives of the United States of America in Congress assembled.'"*

and,

*Title 5, Part 1, Chapter 5, Subchapter 2, Section 552-
Public information; agency rules, opinions, orders,
records, and proceedings:
"(a) Each agency shall make available to the public
information as follows:
(1)(D) substantive rules of general applicability adopted
as authorized by law, and statements of general policy
or interpretations of general applicability formulated and
adopted by the agency;"*

The US House of Representatives' Office of the Law Revision
Counsel observes that of the 50 titles in the US Code, only 1, 3,
4, 5, 9, 10, 11, 13, 14, 17, 18, 23, 28, 31, 32, 35, 36, 37, 38,
39, 44, 46, and 49 have been enacted as positive law, leaving a
27 title majority both un-enacted, and often lacking published
rules for significant sections.

Nonetheless, federal workers issue forth from high-rise
fortresses throughout the country every morning to browbeat
fines, plea bargains and concessions from citizens based upon
those 27 titles, which consist largely of congressional
declarations and executive orders, rather than statutes with
general applicability. (At best, mere portions of those titles are
distorted reflections of older actual statutes).

The fact is, those un-enacted titles are intermingled
with the others, and within each type are intermingled in turn
general statutes and the far more limited declarations and
executive orders mentioned above, which only have application
to federal entities or within federal territorial jurisdiction. This
intermingling makes distinguishing each from the other
extremely difficult-- effectively neutralizing the benefits of form
and notice and leaving most Americans unable to challenge or
resist illegitimate assertions of federal authority. The resultant
passing of practical power from the citizenry to the state, by
default rather than by consent, makes manifest the importance
of respect for *all* the requirements of proper form and notice.

The chief object of the lawful state is to ensure domestic tranquility-- the kind of tranquility which results from the countless conflicts of a free and energetic society having reliable access to an impartial system of resolution and remedy. Such tranquility is not tidy, it is not quiet, and it is not ambitious. It is sheer, resting lightly upon all; and it is flexible, being constructed of values shared by the widest possible divergence of interests. It is as resilient as the laws of nature upon which it is based; and it is as beautiful as the aspirations of individual happiness cherished by each of those it protects. It yields great wealth and power to those who embrace it, but will abide only a light, sober and respectful embrace.

The founders of this great country drew up its plans in the illumination of their understanding of that tranquility and the engine that makes it possible: proper law. Only that particular radiance will reveal how the ongoing project can continue to fit together with the harmony and liberty which are its unique contribution to human weal. Arrogance, ambition, greed and fear all cast long shadows now, but the sharp lines of that great work of genius and humility are still there to be followed if such obstacles can be pushed aside. I hope we all find it in us to lend our weight to the task.

The Sublime Harmonies Of Social Justice In The Upcoming Worker's Paradise
(A Laborious Mental Exercise)
ℰ℧ℭℨ℧ℛ

Imagine that you're a homeowner and over the years you've had some landscaping done to your property: a few decorative trees planted, a stone wall built, a flagstone path installed, etc.. All the work has been done by what had been your favorite contractor, Joe's Landscaping Service.

Joe and his guys have done good work, for the most part, but as time has passed, Joe has been a bit reluctant to invest in new equipment, so his speed has gone down, and his hourly rate has been inching up at the same time. You've brought this to Joe's attention more than once, but he's just shrugged and said, "Hey, a guy's gotta make a living. But I'll try to get the boys to move a little faster."

Eventually, when Joe announces that he's raising his rates yet again you pull out the Yellow Pages and find a new outfit, Sam's Quality Landscaping. The ad claims that Sam has all the latest gear, and a crew of hard workers. You meet with

Sam, and even though his hourly rate is the same as Joe's, Sam is energetic and sharp, and gives you a good feeling about his work ethic. So, you make a deal, and then give Joe a call.

"Don't bother to schedule that re-sodding that we were talking about," you tell Joe, "I'm going to have someone else do it." Joe glares at the phone as he hangs up, and mutters, "We'll see about that!"

*****

Now, imagine that on the day that Sam shows up to start on the project, he finds your driveway blocked by Joe's rig, with Joe and his helpers marching in front of your house, yelling ugly threats at you and your wife and kids. Sam and his crew are promptly made targets of the abuse as well, with Joe loudly calling out, "We're doing this for you, too, you know! You should be here picketing with us, you damn scabs!"

Imagine that when you call the police, a cop arrives, sizes up the situation and smirks, "Sorry, Bub, there's nothin' I can do. You're Joe's customer. You gotta work it out with him."

"What are you talking about?" you protest. "I don't belong to Joe! I can hire whoever I want to work on my yard!" The cop laughs. "This is a union neighborhood, pal." One of Joe's boys hurls a rock through your picture window.

"Hey!" you yell at the cop, "Arrest that guy!"

"Not sure I saw who did that," replies the cop, "and besides, brother Joe and his boys are just trying to protect their jobs."

Eventually, you prevail upon the cop to make Joe move his rig so that Sam and his crew can get in with theirs and start to work. At the end of the day Sam notices that one of the taillights on his truck is smashed and there's a long, deep scratch down its side. As he backs into the street, a tire blows. Seeing Joe and his boys moving toward him, one of them thoughtfully bringing his own tire iron, Sam elects to drive away on the flat, heading down the street with a "whup, whup, whup". Joe and his lads laugh. Sam calls you later that evening and tells you he can't come back until things have settled down. He says he needs the work, but he can't risk his equipment. You tell him you understand.

Early the next morning you roar out of your driveway past the pallets of wilting sod. A couple of Joe's men, yawning and nursing steaming cups of coffee, heave rocks in your direction, but it's early and they're not really trying, so you get away with only one small ding in your trunk lid. You head for the city office, intending to demand some of the police service for which you have been paying taxes all these years. Your salary is going to get docked for taking the time off work, but the sod is already paid for; Sam is counting on the job; and besides, you can't just give in to extortion. When you arrive, you're surprised to find Joe there. A man from the National Labor Relations Board is with him.

"I hope you brought your bank statement and 1040 with you," the bureaucrat says brightly, "so we can get a good idea of what you can afford to pay Joe." Catching sight of the shocked expression on your face, he frowns and says, "Well, you're a private citizen of course, so you don't HAVE to produce the documents; but I'll be obliged to take your lack of cooperation into account when I make my decision about this matter. Furthermore, if we can't work things out and this ends up in court, the judge won't look very favorably on that, either.

Such uncooperativeness suggests you're not really bargaining in good faith"

"I'm not bargaining at all!" you protest. The bureaucrat shakes his head and smiles tightly. "Well, I'm afraid we can't very well have that! Your failing to bargain would almost certainly lead to serious discord in the community."

Just then, one of Joe's men hurries in and whispers in Joe's ear for a moment before turning to you with a grin. "I've just been down to that shop where your wife works," he says. "I told her boss that as long as she and her husband were messing with our jobs, we're going to boycott his business. He was not a happy camper!"

Your face suddenly hot, you scream, "You son of a bitch!" while your hands ball into fists.

"Hey, now," the NLRB agent says to you sternly, "let's keep this civil!"

*****

Weeks later-- exhausted, numb, and defeated-- you take the pen that is handed to you and sign a contract guaranteeing all your landscaping business to Joe for the next three years at his current rates plus automatic 5% annual increases. Joe smiles. "Don't worry, pal," he says, "now we'll get that sod laid pronto!"

"The sod is all dead," you mumble.

"Well, there's more where that came from, right?" All you can do is stare blankly at him. It's suddenly struck you that, under the circumstances, your home-improvement days are over.

You head for what's left of your car in a daze, visions of the Mad Hatter's tea party running through your bruised mind, when Joe asks conversationally, "Say, how's business down at that grocery store where you work?"

Although chatting with Joe would be the last thing you would do if your brain were fully in gear, you answer reflexively. "Okay, but we're expecting a bit of a slowdown. My boss says that with the cost of labor going up lately, we're going to have to raise our prices."

Joe frowns. "Man, that's a drag! I shop there myself. I guess I'll have to find a new store."

A strange light begins to shine in your eyes as what Joe has just said slowly sinks in. With a wicked, satisfied smile you turn to look at him. "Oh yeah? We'll see about that!"

*****

For the record, I fully support the inalienable right of anyone and everyone to associate, combine, and coordinate with anyone else, and to strike at will. However, I also fully support the inalienable right of anyone and everyone to the uncompromised control of their own property; and the right to refuse to associate, combine, and coordinate with anyone else-- which includes the right to decline participation in a union and the right to refuse to enter into contract with anyone or any group.

The Cuban Conundrum
ᔕᦠᏣᏄᎢᏄᎧᏢ

The perennial argument over the long-standing American policy of embargo against Cuba is in the air again lately. This conflict underscores the profitless character of policies which serve political interests [read: pandering] rather than principles.

On the one side are those whose hatred of the Castro regime is so intense and blinding that they cannot abide the idea of any intercourse with Cuba which might obscure the failure of Castro's policies, and who simultaneously embrace the pipe-dream that if only the Cuban people are made sufficiently miserable they will rise up. With sharp-edged farm implements and heavy 1950's auto parts in their desperate hands (goes the fantasy), these long-suffering victims will fall upon the well-fed, well-armed and pampered Praetorian Guard with which Castro keeps them in slavery, and hack and bludgeon their way to glorious freedom. However, seeing that it's been forty years now since the tyrant took power, I think the legitimacy of this expectation is getting rather thin.

On the other are the "constructive engagement" advocates who argue that as a consequence of international trade with Castro's thugs (through whom all business with any entity on the island must flow), the condition of the slave population will be raised to the point at which their burgeoning wealth and habits of consumption and production cause the irresistible ascendancy of liberty-- sort of an alternative version of Marx's "withering away of the state". The mystical process by which this transformation takes place in a country lacking free elections-- and in which the exploited segment of the population possesses no means of enforcing its interest in such elections-- is as yet unidentified, but hey, it could happen, right? The sub-text here is one of flat-eyed realpolitick: This government's not going away anytime soon; the business of business is business, not politics; and there's money to be made on this island, right now.

The pro-embargo view at least recognizes both that America has a moral imperative to scorn a tyrant and cheer the ambitions of the tyrannized, and that nothing will happen without the rising up of the people, however unlikely that may be under the current circumstances; while the anti-embargo crowd, speaking plainly, really doesn't give a damn and wants no policy at all. Doubtless there are head-nodders for "constructive engagement" that are well-meaning and innocently taken in by the title's self-validating declaratory character, but anyone who has spent a few moments considering the matter (as we presume its main boosters have) must know it as a completely empty fraud. The better name for the policy would be "constructive engorgement".

Neither of these approaches can do any real good in Cuba unless the embargo becomes so total that even the elite who defend the regime are weakened with hunger or run out of bullets; or the "constructive engagement" so enriches them that they all abandon the island and move to Switzerland to be closer to their bank accounts. Under both rather optimistic scenarios the normal Cuban continues to suffer long into the future.

So, I'd like to offer a third way for consideration-- one that I think is more in tune with reality, and which also possesses the virtues of both a proven track record and an unquestionable ideological conformity to America's finest political principles. Additionally, it's quick and cheap.

In a nutshell, the idea is this: Escorted by suitable fighter jet support to provide for safe passage, we fly cargo transports over Cuba dropping crates of handguns, assault rifles and ammunition into every village square, plaza, barrio and backyard. We drop some in the woods. We drop some on the beach. We drop some in the hills. We drop them in so many places that the Castro forces can't get to them all before the people do. Then we sit back and watch the power arrangements in Cuba get sorted out.

We'd have to include some instructions, of course. First, some basics on loading and operating the weapons, which should be selected for ruggedness and simplicity. But the more important instructions would be designed to guide the people on how to most effectively seize the moment to their maximum advantage, and that would go something like this:

> 1. Kill anyone who would be upset at the idea of you having a weapon (it is a sure identifier of your oppressors).

> 2. When needed, band with your neighbors to kill anyone trying to disarm any one of you.

3. After all the people interested in disarming you are dead, get together and write a Constitution (and keep the guns).

There. Sound radical? Perhaps, but it isn't actually new-- we did the same thing in occupied France during WW II, dropping "Liberator" handguns behind German lines on little parachutes with simple instructions to the finder about creeping up behind the nearest Nazi and doing what came naturally. It did a lot of good in France, and it would do at least as much in Cuba.

The program would be foreign-aid on a thin dime-- I figure we could gin up 1,000,000 weapons and ammo for no more than 250 million dollars, and even with the aircraft expenses the program would be better than a bargain at twice the price.

Personally, I don't see a downside, even in foreign relations. After all, we'd merely be "empowering the people", a noble purpose to which all governments pay constant and proper homage, at least rhetorically. The only regimes that would really howl would be those whose nightmares involve the same sort of airlift into their countries. Like North Korea, China, Afghanistan...

Hmmmmmm.

We might want to schedule more than one delivery, while we're at it...

The Power Of The Jury
ᔕᏅᏣᏋᏅᏨ

    Two important jury nullification cases were in the papers recently: The California Supreme Court's ruling that nullification, or judgment of the law, was not a power available to a Golden State juror; and the U.S. Supreme Court's refusal to wield it's proudly claimed, but selectively exercised, nullification power in the case of United States v. Oakland Cannabis Buyers Cooperative. In the former case, the court's absurd declaration proves the wisdom of the founders in recognizing that there is an irreducible conflict of interest between the citizenry and any organ of government-- even an allegedly independent judiciary. In the latter, the U.S. Supreme Court abrogates its responsibility to serve as a safeguard against overreach by the legislative and executive branches yet again. By declining to stand in judgment of the law on behalf of the whole nation, in its acknowledged capacity as what amounts to a permanent nullification-equipped jury, the court allows injustice to continue and fosters a corrosive disrespect for the law. Together, the two actions underscore the critical importance of jury nullification as a power available to, and practiced by, 'common' citizens.

The California Supreme Court, in accepting the case of a juror who appealed being thrown off a jury for stating explicitly that he did not intend to deliberate the facts regarding one count of a multi-count indictment because he did not consider the act charged to be criminal, deliberately seized the opportunity to mis-educate Californians about the law (and stick it's foot in it's mouth, to boot). It could have declined to hear the case, but instead arrogantly bulled forward, apparently eager to put us rubes in our place.

Nullification *"may sound lofty,"* Chief Justice Ronald M. George wrote, *"but such unchecked and unreviewable power can lead to verdicts based on bigotry and racism."* The court also warned that nullification would leave the fate of defendants to the *"whims of a particular jury"* which could disregard the presumption of innocence or even convict *"by the flip of a coin."* Perhaps the Chief Justice and the California Supreme Court have forgotten that the jury's real power as regards a defendant is that of acquittal, not of conviction-- an improper or suspect conviction by a jury can be overturned by many reviewing tribunals, as well as the trial judge, but a jury's acquittal is the word of God. That fact alone, acknowledged by even the most ardent foes of jury nullification, proves them wrong, for such uncontestable power, while consistent with a right of nullification, is contradictory with the idea that a jury must be bound by instructions from the court as to the applicability of the law. Were the latter true, a mechanism would exist for overturning a jury's acquittal based on a contest of its compliance with those instructions. (Regarding *"verdicts based on bigotry and racism,"* one can only hope that, upon contemplation of selected instances of legislative action insufficiently checked by jury nullification, the Chief Justice would have the grace to reconsider this remark and glumly eat a bit of Jim Crow).

In the U.S. Supreme Court action, the justices declined to consider the constitutionality of the Controlled Substances Act while ruling that California's Medical Marijuana initiative (legalizing the distribution and use of marijuana by a doctor's prescription) could, under the auspices of that act, essentially be ignored by federal courts and law enforcement agencies. Having been given the chance to dodge the issue (because the appellate court whose ruling was being contested did not explicitly raise the constitutional issue), the Supreme Court cravenly seized it, saying, *"Nor are we passing today on a Constitutional question, such as whether the Controlled Substances Act exceeds Congress' power under the Commerce Clause."*

Article VI of the U. S. Constitution says, *"This Constitution, and the Laws of the United States which shall be made in Pursuance thereof... shall be the supreme Law of the Land; and the Judges in every State shall be bound thereby..."* Clearly, consideration of any aspect of a law by a judge within the U.S.A. must first address the question of constitutionality, for no law which fails that test has any force in this country. It is absurd to spend a moment's time deliberating about fine points of applicability, as the court did in this case-- debating, for instance, the philosophical question of whether the virtues of the defendant's claim of medical necessity could outweigh the public policy virtues asserted by the act's supporters (they held that it did not)-- before, or, in fact, without, determining the foundational validity of the act.

It is obvious that the Controlled Substances Act would, in this case, fail the test. The 'Commerce' clause says, *"Congress shall have the power: To regulate Commerce with foreign Nations, and among the several States, and with the Indian tribes;...."* No nuanced reasoning is required to perceive that even a typically broad, tortured and accommodating reading of this clause cannot empower Congress to legislate over the distribution or use of marijuana grown and consumed in California by Californians, which was the underlying issue in the case at hand. The simple fact is that California's Medical Marijuana initiative was entirely superfluous except in demonstrating how successful have been the efforts of worshippers of government in eroding the general understanding of Constitutional limitations. California should simply have announced as a matter of state policy that DEA agents would no longer be permitted to arrest and prosecute Californians for medical use of marijuana.

With its cramped ruling in this case, the Supreme Court is obviously guilty of dereliction of duty-- having failed to trouble themselves to judge the law, as they are duty bound to do. In this, they lend the weight of their institutional authority to a dangerous misunderstanding of the nature of the law and set a very bad example for other juries in other trials.

A jury's first duty, as representatives of the sovereign citizenry, is to ask itself the questions, *"Do I have the right to hinder another in doing what the accused is charged with?"* and *"Even if I do, is this act really one of those from which we, the people, sought to protect ourselves when we created this government, and if so, is this law-- which will, by the way, be available in future to be wielded against me and mine in turn based upon the precedent set here today-- really an accurate and finely-enough tuned expression of that purpose?"* Only after these questions are decided in the affirmative does the question of whether indeed the accused committed the act charged arise.

The founders recognized that the energy of the state-- always enormously larger and more powerful than that of any one defendant-- will inevitably and irrepressibly be devoted to a proliferation of laws, regulations, and impositions on people's lives, even in the most carefully designed system. As Jefferson observed, *"It is the natural progress of things for government to gain ground, and liberty to yield."* Therefore, in striking the necessary balance between the (reluctantly) acknowledged necessity of government and the provision of sufficient safeguards for the liberty and preservation of individual sovereignty which is its purpose, they placed numerous stumbling blocks in the way of the exercise of state power-- any one of which could serve to shield them and their descendants from its might.

Taken together, these various safeguards-- such as a written constitution authorizing a limited scope to government power; a representative legislature appointed by the citizenry and removable if dissatisfactory; an independent judiciary presumed to have no stake in the outcome of a trial; and, at nearly the last resort, the requirement that a representative sampling of the citizenry must offer its imprimatur of approval before the state may act forcefully against one of their fellows-- are designed to give each and all of us an equitable defense against abuse and tyranny. They ensure that it is the people, not an elite ruling class, that have the final say in how the power of the state can be used.

The true rulers in this country-- the citizens-- are engaged in diverse pursuits and leave much that is done in their name in the hands of their representatives. But, like the master who, while permitting his servant to shop, negotiate, and even write the check, wisely reserves to himself the authority to sign and thus commit to the decision, the people reserve to themselves the final authority in the application of force, by means of the power and purpose of the jury. As a representative of the law-making community as a whole, it is the juror's own law that is proposed to be applied, and so it is unquestionably within his authority to consider the virtue and purpose of that law one last time before it is brought to bear.

It is the state's conceit that the constitutional mechanisms of a democratically elected legislature and an allegedly independent judiciary are themselves sufficient safeguards by virtue of which the fitness of all laws, as ultimately brought to bear, can be relied upon. But the founders were not so arrogant as to presume that those mechanisms were perfect in design, unsusceptible to subversion, incapable of misunderstanding, or proof against the ascension to power of the corrupt, and therefore needed no further checks upon the application of community power. Thus, recognizing that government is, as George Washington is reputed to have said, *"Like fire-- a dangerous servant and a fearful master,"* they blessed us with the potential inconveniences of too much liberty, seen rightly as infinitely preferable to those attending too little of it.

After all, the harm that can be done by one citizen even if unwisely free by the decision of his fellows into (after all) their own midst, is immeasurably less than that which might be accomplished by a government not kept tightly reined-in and susceptible to overrule should it seek to stray. Keeping those reins firmly in hand, in principle and in practice, is among our chief civic responsibilities, careful attention to which is owed both to our own interest and to that of our posterity.

"It is not only his [the juror's] right, but his duty . . . to find the verdict according to his own best understanding, judgment, and conscience, though in direct opposition to the directions of the court."
-John Adams

"I consider trial by jury as the only anchor yet imagined by man by which a government can be held to the principles of its Constitution."
-Thomas Jefferson

"The jury has the right to judge both the law as well as the fact in controversy."
-John Jay

"The friends and adversaries of the plan of the [Constitutional] convention, if they agree on nothing else, concur at least in the value they set upon the trial by jury; or if there is any difference between them it consists of this: the former regard it as a valuable safeguard to liberty, the latter represent it as the very palladium of free government."
-Alexander Hamilton

"If it [jury power] is not law, it is better than law, it ought to be law, and will always be law wherever justice prevails."
-Ben Franklin

"A nation of sheep begets a government of wolves."
-Edward R. Murrow

An Unreasonable Assault On The Fourth
ℰ൦ᘓℰ൦ᘓ

"Necessity is the plea for every infringement of human freedom.
It is the argument of tyrants; it is the creed of slaves."
-William Pitt

    The Supreme Court heard arguments in 2001 in a
significant case testing the limits of warrantless searches, a
degenerate abuse of police power becoming increasingly
common under the auspices of the 'War on Drugs', and the 'War
on Terrorism'. The immediate issue was the use of an infrared
sensor by police to remotely explore the home of one Danny
Lee Kyllo, suspected of growing marijuana indoors, without the
benefit of a warrant. The infrared sensor registers the
emanations of heat from the object of its attention, and the
growing of plants indoors (whether marijuana or any other)
requires the extensive use of high output lights, which shed a
lot of heat. No particular justification, such as immediacy of
need, was a factor in the police's failure to seek a warrant; they
just didn't think they had to bother, and indeed, the use of such
sensing devices without judicial oversight is widespread among
police departments. The practice is felt to fall under the 'plain

view' doctrine, whereby the courts have held that whatever a citizen presents to public view or access, or fails to take steps to conceal, is fair game for police examination on what amounts to the whim of the officer.

Although originally more modest, the 'plain view' doctrine has been promiscuously expanded by application of a 'reasonable expectation of privacy' standard in defining what 'plain view' means. This standard, as its name suggests, transforms 'plain view' into a subjective and evolving concept. Thus, the 'plain view' concept, which used to be most widely applied to the picking through of garbage put out on the street, is increasingly being relied upon in the defense of forms of surveillance unanticipated when it was first conceived.

It will be called upon, for instance, to counter challenges to the use of 'sniffers', which test exhalations for the presence of alcohol, a device increasingly popular with police traffic units, and deployed without either the knowledge of the subject or any prior finding of probable cause or even reasonable suspicion. They are simply applied at every traffic stop. The theory is that in exhaling, a citizen has willingly offered the contents of his or her bloodstream for public analysis, waiving all expectations of privacy. Those seeking to establish a sufficient legal basis for the assertion of their right to privacy are advised to refrain from such wanton indiscretions.

In the Kyllo case, the state suggested that if Mr. Kyllo wished to enjoy any reasonable expectation of privacy, he should have lined his home with heat shields in order to prevent government agents from peering within. In so doing, the state is essentially arguing a fundamentally corrupt intellectual palindrome to the effect that only upon directing its devices at Kyllo's home and failing to detect what it thought it might did it become possible to establish (or needful to consider) that it lacked justification to have looked in the first place?!

Actually, of course, the state denies the need to paste even so contrived a fig-leaf over its behavior. The position of the state is that the police have the authority to search you or your home by every means short of physical entry whether cause can be cited or not, per the 'plain view/reasonable expectation' concept. For instance, it has lately become 'reasonable' for Americans to expect to be frisked (albeit electronically) every time they prepare to board a plane or enter many buildings-- a procedure which is being upgraded to X-raying in some cases.

Likewise, officially-recognized 'reasonable expectations' have evolved (or devolved) as law enforcement has embraced such practices as flying over remote private property while deploying high-powered optics; installing cameras and ultra sensitive microphones on city streets; and watching activity on citizens computers via remote devices that read electromagnetic emanations from monitors (along with devices like the 'sniffers' and infrared sensors previously discussed); all without warrants or probable cause. Reflect on what could be said to be the 'reasonable expectation of privacy' of a North Korean, to get a good perspective on the potential of this moving-target dynamic. But don't worry; be happy. The innocent have nothing to fear.

Considered from any perspective other than abject submission to government contemptuous of its proper limits, the entire foundational concept of 'reasonable expectation' is absurd and indefensible. In a Constitutional system of government in which the Fourth Amendment is a part of the supreme law of the land, a 'reasonable expectation of privacy' comprises an expectation that your person, house, papers and effects will be utterly free of direct contemplation *in any form* by the law-enforcement agencies of government unless probable cause sufficient to satisfy an independent (and, theoretically, skeptical) judge has been previously established by other means, the only exception being in times of immediate danger. In other words, *an expectation of scrupulous respect, on the part of all state actors, for both the letter and the spirit of the Fourth Amendment.* The only alternative is the corrupt circular argument discussed earlier.

*****

Since the advent of the 'War on Terror', yet another government effort to exploit the inherent slipperiness of the term 'reasonable' has found favor with those to whom the conveniences of the state are more important than the liberties (and clearly expressed instructions) of those who created the institution in the first place. This attempt to escape the bonds of the Fourth Amendment is a far more egregious offense than even the grossly cynical 'reasonable expectation of privacy' argument, as it involves the deliberate misconstruction of an eminently demonstrable truth regarding the meaning of the amendment. It has seen recent prominent expressions in an appellate panel's overruling of the refusal of a secret Foreign Intelligence Surveillance Act oversight court to permit wider license to the Justice Department in wiretapping Americans without a warrant; and in the Pentagon's initiative to track and record information on all activities of all Americans-- originally unveiled as the 'Total Information Awareness' program, but put back in the closet after a properly outraged and horrified public reaction.

Both the appellate panel's dicta, and the Pentagon's defense of its program, attempt to capitalize upon the presence of the word 'unreasonable' in the text of the Fourth Amendment. The argument offered is that the Fourth Amendment should be understood as prohibiting only 'unreasonable' searches and seizures without a warrant. Thus (the argument proceeds), warrantless searches are permitted, as long as they are 'reasonable'. (No explanation is offered for why an 'unreasonable' search or seizure should be provided for under any circumstances...)

This specious argument continues a durable tradition. Enthusiasts for a promiscuous expansion of state police power always deploy one or another version of the claim that, "*... the Constitution makes clear that the scope of our rights is reduced during crises"*, and characterize the Fourth Amendment as particularly fragile in this respect-- in utter (or willful) ignorance of both its context, its construction, and simple logic.

In this regard, these advocates propose that the inclusion of 'unreasonable' in the amendment means not only that 'unreasonable' searches are permitted as long as they are conducted with a warrant, and that 'reasonable' searches need no warrant-- but also that the amendment's governance of the state operates on a sliding scale, by virtue of which what is 'unreasonable' can and should diminish in an inverse relationship to the magnitude of the current crisis. To a population largely ignorant of the history behind the Fourth Amendment, and accustomed to viewing all law as a mystery, these proposals sound superficially plausible. Nonetheless, they are completely contrary to the facts. The Founder's intention in providing the Fourth Amendment was to recognize that *any* search or seizure which did not conform to the standards of both probable cause attested to under oath, and specificity as to object, was *inherently* unreasonable. They constructed the amendment in order to ensure that no search or seizure would ever take place without a warrant, and that all warrants under which searches and seizures were authorized conformed to the standards provided.

After all, the Fourth, in addition to embodying the fundamental character of the proper relationship between government and citizen, was erected in response to a particular practice of the English government against the pre-revolutionary colonists: The issuance of what were known as 'general warrants', under which agents of the government exercised the power to poke through the property, papers and effects of citizen at the whim of the government, based upon any handy pretext. Such general warrants were identical in character to those sought by today's Justice Department and Pentagon (and others) based upon this assertion of a 'reasonableness' exception in the Fourth.

The Fourth Amendment reads as follows, *"The right of the people to be secure in their persons, houses, papers, and effects, against unreasonable searches and seizures, shall not be violated, and no Warrants shall issue, but upon probable cause, supported by Oath or affirmation, and particularly describing the place to be searched, and the persons or things to be seized."* While I will grant that its construction could be slightly improved with the addition of a period after "*violated*" and the removal of the following "*and*", this would only be an improvement because it would make more difficult its willful distortion by apologists for the state. But modification is not necessary. Plenty of evidence as to the meaning of the Amendment is readily at hand.

For instance, the Virginia Declaration of Rights, one of the earlier versions of the Fourth upon which the federal Constitutional amendment was modeled, reads in pertinent part,

> *"That general warrants, whereby any officer or messenger may be commanded to search suspected places without evidence of a fact committed, or to seize any person or persons not named, or whose offence is not particularly described and supported by evidence, are grievous and oppressive, and ought not to be granted".*

Similarly, the Declaration of Rights in the Pennsylvania Constitution of 1776, another precursor to the Fourth, says,

"That the people have a right to hold themselves, their houses, papers, and possessions free from search and seizure, and therefore warrants without oaths or affirmations first made, affording a sufficient foundation for them, and whereby any officer or messenger may be commanded or required to search suspected places, or to seize any person or persons, his or their property, not particularly described, are contrary to that right, and ought not to be granted".

James Madison, in arguing for the inclusion of the Bill of Rights before Congress, described his intent for the Fourth thusly:

"The rights of the people to be secured in their persons; their houses, their papers, and their other property, from all unreasonable searches and seizures, shall not be violated by warrants issued without probable cause, supported by oath or affirmation, or not particularly describing the places to be searched, or the persons or things to be seized".

That he meant that it was OK that such rights be violated as long as no warrant was involved-- which is what the 'reasonable' exception argument really amounts to-- is absurd.

Massachusetts, in its Constitution of 1780, put it this way:

"Every subject has a right to be secure from all unreasonable searches, and seizures of his person, his houses, his papers, and all his possessions. All warrants, therefore, are contrary to this right, if the cause or foundation of them be not previously supported by oath or affirmation; and if the order in the warrant to a civil officer, to make search in suspected places, or to arrest one or more suspected persons, or to seize their property, be not accompanied with a special designation

*of the persons or objects of search, arrest, or seizure:
and no warrant ought to be issued but in cases, and
with the formalities, prescribed by the laws".*

Thus, the record makes clear, to all except those who
do not wish to understand, that by virtue of the Fourth
Amendment, the federal government is denied the power to
conduct warrantless searches or seizures under any
circumstances; and that those conducted by means of a warrant
must conform to the careful prescriptions of probable cause
previously established under penalty of perjury, and particularity
and explicitness as to the evidence to be sought and seized.

The idea is simple... the power of the state is great and
onerous to counter, and citizens should be spared having to
bear the stress of its regard, and of having to defend
themselves against its allegations, unless justifications
convincing to an objective arbiter are at hand. This is the first
and most significant aspect of the principle of *"presumed
innocent until proven guilty"*. That there is a point at which a
search of the likeliest place in which the state has probable
cause to believe particularly identified evidence of a crime exists
is undoubted. However, to suggest that anyone can be
subjected to the state's scrutiny based on anything less than
probable cause is to embrace an opposite principle: That no
one is presumed innocent until they have been proven so.

It is no coincidence that 'evolving' (that is to say,
lawless) standards, and the reliance on arguments which
attempt to lift themselves by their own bootstraps, have become
the preferred devices of the state in recent decades. The
adoption of-- or rather, dependency upon-- these devices
parallels the expansion of the general concept of 'Crimes
Against the State', a class of offense characterized most
essentially by the lack of a victim.

That this is so can be made clear by simply considering the way in which a warrant is commonly obtained in a by-the-book fashion: As a consequence of a victim's sworn complaint and accusation; or by the examination of a crime scene and the generation of a list of suspects based upon physical and/or testimonial evidence found thereby-- either of which amounts to independent evidence to be presented to a judge. It's not tricky or difficult...

On the other hand, when the nature of the 'offense' is disobedience to some state directive, and thus involves no complainant, these precursor elements by which warrants are legitimately justified are typically not available. In such cases the natural inclination of related law enforcement efforts is toward proactive scrutiny of the citizenry in search of indications of guilt. Such police attention is, of course, inherently arbitrary and capricious-- necessarily taking place *before* the existence of any probable cause, and being largely indiscriminate in its application. But it is often only by such practices that victimless behavior can be detected and punished. (The testimony of unsolicited informants can provide for exceptions to this rule, of course, but could hardly be relied upon to suffice for broad and meaningful enforcement of a directive targeting the general population; furthermore, when such testimony is available, a warrant will be, too.)

The simple fact is that regardless of what pretexts might be deployed in an effort at its justification, the assault on the Fourth Amendment is not in service to any necessity of crisis, or even merely an attempt to compromise between the rights of Americans and some interest in 'law and order'. It is, rather, an assault on behalf of the exercise of arbitrary dictatorial authority by the state, to which the Fourth, when properly understood, stands as a formidable obstacle.

*****

It is the foolish vanity of those who believe that their interests are being served by today's erosion of liberty to think that they will not pay the price tomorrow. Power is a hungry beast, and as it grows, so does its appetite. Bourne observed that *"War is the health of the state"* meaning that by capitalizing on a condition or sense of crisis the State expands its power with the approval of the anxious and frightened people. Today, the 'War On Drugs' and the 'War on Terror' are the crises of the hour, and the treatments (no cures appear to be available) are proving predictably worse than the diseases. Tomorrow, another necessity will demand another mandate, and while the state will thus seek more new powers, those ceded in this present 'crisis' will not be relinquished.

For that matter, one would think that even those in government who advocate a doctrine of exceptions to the supremacy and clarity of the Constitution in times of crisis would fear that such a doctrine would rob them of their power and authority, both entirely dependent upon that supreme charter for legitimacy. But, of course, this is mere sarcasm. Those occupying positions of power mean to wield power regardless, without much concern about legitimacy, and so have no trepidations. That being so, a little concern on the part of the rest of us might not be unreasonable.

*****

P.S. The Supreme Court ruled in the Kyllo case at the end of 2001:

> *Held: Where, as here, the Government uses a device that is not in general public use, to explore details of a private home that would previously have been unknowable without physical intrusion, the surveillance is a Fourth Amendment "search," and is presumptively unreasonable without a warrant.*

'K' is for Kids... and Kleptocrats
ℰ☯ℭℬ☯ℭℛ

November 5th is shaping up to be a typical special interest feeding frenzy as voters across the nation are besieged with an assortment of pleas for subsidies from the usual crowd of welfare-mongers, some freshly minted and others warmed-over by the never-take-no-for-an-answer types. Here in Southeastern Michigan, voters in two Detroit-area counties are being asked for the second (or is it the third?) time to approve an "arts" tax by which local entertainment operations of considerable interest to a certain elite segment of the population will be paid for by a not-so-elite, and only moderately and variably interested segment of the population. Ostensibly, the scheme will facilitate access to these operations by a third, indigent poster-child segment of the population, one which actually has no interest in them whatsoever.

Really, the purpose is to spare the elite segment from being pestered by these operations for funding, and to spare the operations themselves from having to charge ticket prices reflective of their high expenses and low market share. Such realistic pricing would further marginalize their already scant traffic and reveal unmistakably that, at least as currently constituted, these operations lack any meaningful general utility.

As is characteristic of such pandering, the effort by SE Michigan's cultural elite to finance its personal interests with its neighbor's money is cloyingly titled "Proposal K- Metropolitan Arts and Culture Council- Arts, Parks, and Kids Millage Proposal". It seeks to extract $46,000,000.00 per year from property owners in two out of the three area counties, two thirds of which is to "support programming for children, families and seniors" by being disbursed to "non-profit regional history, science, and arts institutions and local arts and recreation programs within its operating area of Oakland County and Wayne County". (The other third of the money would be kicked back to each little village, township, and city within the two counties to fund local politician's pet projects. Guess which way those folks will vote.)

All of this language is the standard boilerplate deployed ad nauseum by thieves tarting themselves up as national treasures, accented with a general issue, "They're-Too-Stupid-To-Know- What's-Good-For-Them" ambience. That subtext motivates and describes both a certain morally and economically confused, but well-meaning, segment of the electorate, which suspects that it may be part of the "They" and feels guilty and shamed; and many of their smug, supercilious and self-centered neighbors who, equally confused but imagining themselves part of the intelligentsia and actively supporting the tax, are completely unsuspecting.

One of the charms of this element of the con is that there is a one-to-one correspondence between the degree to which the subtext is true and the futility of the proposed subsidy solution. Even if we grant the value of the benefiting institution's offerings, *those who are too stupid to know what is good for them will not patronize the institutions and programs regardless of the degree to which they are subsidized. If they would, the subsidies are unnecessary.* A further delightful irony is that it is largely the efforts-- denigrating and 'deconstructing' all established standards of value in the schools and mainstream media that they control and influence-- of those smug and supercilious types who are sure that their neighbors fall into the "...Too-Stupid-To Know..." category that has indeed left many too ignorant to know what is *good,* whether for them or otherwise.

*****

The "non-profit" regional history, science and art institutions which will receive the lion's share of the money consist of several specific Detroit-located museums that are manifestly unable to draw enough traffic at competitive prices to pay their own freight, and thus to possess much of a reason for being. They seek to trade on sympathy by passing themselves off as struggling to keep their doors open just for the good of the community, and purely out of the generosity of the enlightened spirits of their staffs.

Of course, in reality their "non-profit" status is indistinguishable from that of any plumber in the normal sense of the term, unless the plumber is a publicly-traded, dividend-distributing corporation. It is only in the looking-glass world of the IRS that any difference exists, and then only because of that happy organization's systematic mischaracterization of the plumber's business. Both the plumber and the museum staff are just individuals, or collections of individuals, who work for a paycheck-- and very handsome paychecks in the case of the museums. Although I have been unable to secure exact numbers for Detroit area institutions, 'The Art Newspaper' reports that, as of 2001, U.S. museum director's salaries range as high as $505,797.00, with bonuses of as high as an additional 1.7 million dollars. The mean salary for such positions (based on surveys of institutions with annual operating budgets of $1.6 million or more) is $160,130.00, plus bonuses, benefits, and, usually, housing; with presumable proportionality for subordinate positions. Not bad action for starry-eyed non-profiteers. The motivations which inspire these institutions should not be confused with those of Mother Teresa.

*****

It is reassuring to know that the programming which is to be supported targets "children" as well as "families"; otherwise one would be left to conclude that the "family" programming will extend no further than marriage encounters, or sex clinics, although the casual observer might be forgiven for imagining that the inclusion of "Kids" in the proposal's title renders the "children" in the description a superfluity. Such an observer, exhibiting thereby a complete naiveté regarding the virtue of buzzwords in practical politics, doubtless is among the "Too-Stupid..." segment which so badly needs the counsel of others in the area of cultural budgeting.

Taking that description at face value, one must conclude that single, under 65 adults are going to get unabashedly screwed by this deal, as they are glaringly omitted from the list of targeted beneficiaries. That demographic is less likely to vote than the parent and senior crowd, who are being invited to cadge a passel of goodies at their expense, so I don't doubt that the omission is deliberate and cunning.

On the other hand Macomb county, the third of the three counties making up central metropolitan Detroit and sure to take as much advantage of subsidized core-city institutions as their neighbors, gets a free pass, having opted out of the proposal. They declined the opportunity to try coat-tailing some local pelf on the Save Our Beloved Museums scheme, and will keep all of their money in their own pockets regardless of the outcome of the vote. Apparently even a district that incomprehensibly re-elected David Bonior to Congress for years and years enjoys an occasional lapse into sanity.

*****

The institutions which would receive the subsidies sought with this proposal have already been donated or pledged, and have spent much of, some $500,000,000.00 over the past couple of years, and still can't draw enough trade to make ends meet (at least at the style to which they are accustomed). Even the ferociously promoted 12-week-long Van Gogh exhibit two years ago at the Detroit Institute of Arts (the flagship of the local "arts community"), hailed as overwhelmingly the most successful exhibit in the museum's history, pulled only 315,000 visitors. At first glance this appears to be a large number. However, consider that thousands upon thousands of tickets to the show were given away free by the museum (around 60,000-- virtually all to local attendees); a very large percentage of the total attendance was from outside of the area; and the metropolitan area population exceeds 4.7 million (more than 3.2 million of which is concentrated in the two targeted counties). It thus becomes clear that fewer than 5% of the people who would be taxed under Proposal K bothered to attend even this "must-see blockbuster" event, and considerably fewer than that actually paid to do so.

When all is said and done, if they can't make it without a gun to someone's head, it would be best to have the art museums make high-resolution scans of all of their inventory available for down-load from the internet, with the actual art going into permanent, controlled-environment storage; and to convert the science museums into public parking garages, prominently adorned with signage directing interested parties to vendors from whom DVD's of "The Magic School Bus" and "Bill Nye The Science Guy" episodes can be bought. The art would thus be even more accessible than it is now; and kids will gain a far more comprehensive and permanent understanding of scientific principles from these commercial productions-- which are detailed, entertaining and can be re-viewed as needed-- than they will ever get from seeing a Jacob's ladder (or whatever) accompanied by a placard with a two paragraph explanation once or twice a year. (And the city desperately needs the parking).

*****

Frederic Bastiat said, "The State is that great fiction by which everyone tries to live at everyone else's expense". On November 5th, as on every other first Tuesday of that month in even numbered years, a lot of people all over the country will join with Detroit's museum gang to prove him right, by trying to climb onto their neighbor's back, whip in hand. Not content with the revenue generated by genuine and voluntary interest in their products, they want to command revenue, on pain of imprisonment, from those with no interest in-- or even an active dislike for-- their wares. Each parasitic effort typically seeks to impose a small burden, but added together, those that have succeeded already extract better than 40% of most citizen's revenue.

Personally, I like museums. I don't visit them often-- I have to work a lot of hours to pay all the taxes by which my parasites are fed. But if I had more time, I'd happily pay a reasonable ticket price to see a good exhibit. For instance, although I doubt I'll live long enough, I'm keeping my hopes alive to someday see one titled something like this-- *"One Thousand-And-One Cons By Which Fast-Talking Scoundrels Screw Their Neighbors-- A Retrospective on Abandoned Political Practices"*.

Gun Control and the Federal Government
ഇ രു രു

"The Constitution shall never be construed... to prevent the people of the United States who are peaceable citizens from keeping their own arms."
-Samuel Adams, Architect of the American Revolution

Over the past half century, meaningful instruction in civics and history (along with much else) has been largely abandoned at virtually all public, and many private, schools. This has created fertile ground for the implantation and spread of a host of falsehoods about the nature, purpose, and particulars of the U.S. Constitution-- an opportunity which has been seized upon and greedily exploited by clients of state power in service to their various interests. One particularly persistent and pernicious such falsehood concerns the meaning of the Second Amendment-- asserting that the amendment tolerates, or even explicitly supports, federal involvement in the area of individual possession of weapons by citizens of the several States. Happily, even a rudimentary (but accurate and rational) analysis of the plain language and historical context of the Constitution, and the Supreme Court jurisprudence on the subject, readily reveals this assertion to be complete nonsense.

It is abundantly clear from as little as a casual study that the Founding Fathers were not foolish or presumptuous enough to believe that they had created a form of government so perfect as to have, in and of itself, offered the people complete protection from usurpation, abuse, or tyranny. Instead, clearly recognizing and wisely fearing the inevitable tendency of all forms of government to seek ever greater control and power, the Founders girded the citizenry about with numerous safeguards of their liberties, intending thereby to ensure that the people always possess the means to remain masters of the relationship. These include the distribution of power among the three competing branches of government; the limited grant of power of any kind as delineated in the written constitution; the provision that laws be subject to a jury's approval each time they are applied; and a series of explicit prohibitions of legislation in certain areas, embodied throughout the Constitution and particularly in the Bill of Rights.

It is acknowledged without dissent that nine of these ten original amendments amount to unambiguous prohibitions of government action, either through expressly forbidding legislation relating to the subject involved, or by expressly dictating the form and limitations of permitted government action. Yet, to the Second Amendment-- clearly the one intended to ensure the retention by the people of the means to enforce upon a balky government obedience to all the rest-- those who see themselves benefiting from the power of the state ascribe a uniquely contrary character. Here, it is argued, is the odd amendment whose purpose is to *authorize* a power of the state, namely that of arming the militia! (With characteristic contempt for the inconveniences of rationality and consistency, the very ideologues who view the federal government as able to claim any authority toward which it may be tempted-- in utter defiance of the doctrine of enumerated powers-- would have this be one power that had to be spelled out, so as to imply that it must belong to the government rather than to the People.)

Even if the obvious incongruity of that were not enough, the government is, in fact, provided with all necessary authority for defense purposes elsewhere. The Constitution-- not a document fraught with redundancies (in fact, the prohibition of unapportioned direct taxation is the only element stated twice)-- specifically authorizes Congress to arm the militia in Article 1, Section 8: *"The Congress shall have Power...To provide for organizing, arming, and disciplining the Militia..."*. Thus, the only *credible* reason for an acknowledgement of the right of the People to keep and bear arms in the Bill of Rights is to preserve it for use against the government whose abridgement of that right is anticipated and prohibited thereby-- in perfect consistency with the character of its fellows.

The willfulness of the 'misunderstanding' suffered by those intent upon violating the amendment is revealed in the single misguided Supreme Court ruling cited in defense of their position:

> *"...The Constitution as originally adopted granted to the Congress power- 'To provide for calling forth the Militia to execute the Laws of the Union, suppress Insurrections and repel Invasions; To provide for organizing, arming, and disciplining, the Militia, and for governing such Part of them as may be employed in the Service of the United States, reserving to the States respectively, the Appointment of the Officers, and the Authority of training the Militia according to the discipline prescribed by Congress.' U.S.C.A.Const. art. 1, 8. With obvious purpose to assure the continuation and render possible the effectiveness of such forces the declaration and guarantee of the Second Amendment were made. It must be interpreted and applied with that*

end in view." United States v. Miller, 307 U.S. 174 (1939) (Emphasis added).

It could be "obvious" only to an idiot that the Second Amendment was added to the Constitution in order to render possible, by prohibiting certain acts of Congress, the exercise of a power with which Congress is explicitly and unambiguously equipped elsewhere. Are we to understand that this is to ensure that the government doesn't find itself in the conundrum of calling forth the militia and then discovering that by virtue of some law that it has itself passed and is unable to repeal, infringing the right to keep and bear arms, the militia must remain unarmed and thus ineffective? Please.

The only interpretation of this reasoning that even approaches making sense is both absurd and contrary to the spin that gun control advocates would have of it: That the Second Amendment *obliges* the people to equip themselves with arms and will thus be ready should the militia be called upon by Congress. Obviously the amendment does not require anyone to keep and bear arms, so it would fail in that purpose, and if that *is* the purpose it is clear thereby that the Founders intended for everyone to possess military weapons (assault rifles, anyone?). But this was not the Founders intent. Their intent was that everyone who *wanted to* should possess weapons, and without any federal interference, so that if the *people*-- whether in their original and supreme capacity as sovereign individuals, or through one or more of their aggregate personas (the several States)-- should call forth the militia, they would not find that it had been hobbled by the enemy.

The Miller decision has other problems, as well. It suffers by virtue of the fundamental issue with which the case is concerned, the possession of a particular type of firearm on which a tax had not been paid. We don't, after all, permit ourselves to be taxed in the exercise of our rights. To impose a tax burden upon the exercise of a right is to infringe upon that right. This is clearly improper and illegal.

Furthermore, the court in Miller makes the error of proposing to classify certain types of weapons as outside of the scope of the amendment:

> *"In the absence of any evidence tending to show that possession or use of a 'shotgun having a barrel of less than eighteen inches in length' at this time has some reasonable relationship to the preservation or efficiency of a well regulated militia, we cannot say that the Second Amendment guarantees the right to keep and bear such an instrument. Certainly it is not within judicial notice that this weapon is any part of the ordinary military equipment or that its use could contribute to the common defense".*

What may or may not be "within judicial notice" is entirely immaterial. It is not within the proper power of the body to whom an infringement is prohibited to determine, or even debate, what objects such a prohibition encompasses. To have it otherwise would make for a porous and meaningless prohibition. This is not to say that such distinctions cannot be made-- they simply cannot be made by, or on behalf of, the prohibited party.

We can leave for another day the question of how the enumeration of the Right to keep and bear arms impacted on the State governments, although I will point out that the Right is reserved, properly, to THE PEOPLE, not the States. Political entities have no rights, only powers and authorities delegated to them by individuals. It suffices, for purposes of this discussion, that it be understood that the Second Amendment removes all matters relating to privately held weapons from the purview of the federal government. All Supreme Court rulings prior to the incomprehensible Miller case acknowledge this fact, and in all cases since the court has never addressed the issue. Rather, the court has confined its rulings on any subsequent gun cases to issues related to the tax or commerce camouflage under cover of which Congress has attempted to evade the amendment's restrictions. Relevant language in the only cases in which the nature and scope of the Second Amendment are explicitly addressed is as follows:

> *"[The Right to Keep and Bear Arms] is not a right granted by the Constitution. Neither is it in any manner dependent upon that instrument for its existence. The second amendment declares that it shall not be infringed; but this, as has been seen, means no more than that it shall not be infringed by Congress. This is one of the amendments that has no other effect than to restrict the powers of the national government,...".* U.S. v. Cruikshank Et Al. 92 U.S. 542 (1875).

> *"We think it clear that the sections under consideration, which only forbid bodies of men to associate together as military organizations, or to drill or parade with arms in cities and towns unless authorized by law, do not infringe the right of the people to keep and bear arms. But a conclusive answer to the contention that this amendment prohibits the legislation in question lies in the fact that the amendment is a limitation only upon the power of congress and the national government, and not upon that of the state".* Presser v. State of Illinois, 116 U.S. 252 (1886).

The court reiterates this same point in Logan v. U.S., 144 U.S. 263 (1892)

There are no other cases specifically addressing the nature, meaning, and scope of the Second Amendment. It is instructive that there are so few. The nation and the courts obviously considered it a clear and unambiguous element of the Constitution, needing no clarification-- as indeed it is.

Contrary to what is popularly believed today, the attitude toward government reflected in the Constitution did not proceed from the immediate experience of the colonists with King George. Rather, it is an expression of their understanding of fundamental power dynamics and the nature of rights and human relations, which had been widely explored in print by such thinkers as John Locke and Adam Smith, and long codified in English and American common law and practice. Some of these principles are: That power belongs to individuals, who cede what they will of it by voluntary consent-- temporarily and on good behavior-- to a collective entity in order to make efficient the defense of their interests; that rights are inherent and inalienable (which is to say, incapable of being made inoperative), and that they exist as a corollary of being human without any government contribution to their legitimacy or character; and that centralized power is by its nature corrupting of those who administer it. The proper understanding of the plain words of the Second Amendment is completely consistent with these principles.

Mao once observed that power flows from the barrel of a gun. Our Founding Fathers, having reclaimed power over their lives and fortunes with armed resistance to government, knew the truth of that observation, and committed themselves to the jealous safeguarding of control by the people over that power, in anticipation of the future. "...Whenever any form of government becomes destructive of these ends, it is the right of the People to alter or abolish it...", says the Declaration of Independence, and the charter subsequently written by the warriors who actualized those powerful words specifically provided themselves and their descendants with the means to do it again, if necessary.

Even simple practicality reveals the rightness of the Founder's genius. No number of madmen, drug dealers, domestic abusers, angry schoolkids, felons, or any other private citizens run amok have ever-- or could ever-- compete with even the smallest and mildest unchecked dictatorial government in creating misery, tragedy, and wholesale death for its citizens. Governments unhindered by the power of forcible resistance from their victims commit their murders by the millions. Is there one person today who would not give their eyeteeth to push a magic button and retroactively arm all of the Jews of 1930's Germany with nice, high capacity assault rifles? Within our own recent memory, the former Soviet Union demanded the surrender of all privately held firearms from Lithuanians when that former subject State began its early talk of independence. And surely the Chinese Communist government rested a great deal easier during the Tiannamen Square demonstrations knowing that the students were unarmed.

Despite the celebration by the left of U.S. v. Miller, Congress has made clear that it recognizes the *"rendering possible its arming of the Militia"* sophistry deployed in that ruling to be the nonsense that it is. The (actually very few) federal restrictions on firearms that *have* been written into statutes invoke some pretext other than a tortured reading of the Second Amendment, such as an exercise of authority under the Commerce Clause or, as was at issue in the Miller case itself, a tax act. That such restrictions are intended to effectively disregard (if not contravene) the Second Amendment can hardly be doubted; nonetheless, Congress does not attempt to justify them by means of the amendment itself.

Further, that the Supreme Court remains cognizant of the Second Amendment's true meaning, and that the Miller ruling was a complete, and subsequently repudiated, aberration, is also clear. The court's summary of case particulars in Tot v. United States, 319 US 463 (1943), illustrates this latter fact nicely:

> *"Both courts below held that the offense created by the Act is confined to the receipt of firearms or ammunition*

as a part of interstate transportation and does not extend to the receipt, in an intrastate transaction, of such articles which, at some prior time, have been transported interstate. The Government agrees that this construction is correct. There remains for decision the question of the power of Congress to create the presumption which 2(f) declares, namely, that, from the prisoner's prior conviction of a crime of violence and his present possession of a firearm or ammunition, it shall be presumed (1) that the article was received by him in interstate or foreign commerce, and (2) that such receipt occurred subsequent to July 30, 1938, the effective date of the statute."

The high court agrees that the statutory authority of the Federal Firearms Act extends only to punishing the personal involvement in an interstate firearms transaction by a convicted felon, not the mere possession by such a person of firearms which had traveled in interstate commerce at some point. It goes on to rule that the government's contention that the accused in such a case should bear the burden of proving that his possession of the firearm was not as a consequence of his own involvement in its interstate transport was unsound, and reverses the conviction of one of the defendants in this combined case, and affirms the appellate court reversal of the trial court conviction of the other.

Similarly, in 1995, in United States v. Lopez (514 US 549), the court again overruled a promiscuous Commerce Clause-based extension of federal firearms authority, striking down the "Gun Free School Zone" act, which purported to prohibit civilian possession of guns within 1000 feet of a school. In the ruling, the court declares that the supposed authority to so legislate under the auspices of the Commerce Clause defies all reason, as firearm possession has no real connection with interstate commerce.

These rulings do not, of course, indicate the court's recognition that *any* such pretext is simply and readily trumped by the clear and explicit directive of the Second Amendment. Still, the impatience with imaginative Congressional and Executive efforts which they *do* reflect offers welcome reassurance that, occasional missteps notwithstanding, the Supreme Court is not prepared to join the other branches of government in a dereliction of duty toward the people's right to keep and bear arms.

Assaults on the plain meaning of the U.S. Constitution, such as the arguments pressed by the government in the Miller case, and the others discussed above, have become a steady rain during the last hundred years, and have taken a creative turn on more fronts than just the right to keep and bear arms. In many cases, the clamor for change is motivated by good intentions (though as often mere sloth and greed are the driving forces). But we must never forget that the Founders looked deep, and recognized that while perhaps the immediate ends-- and actors-- behind a relaxation of restraints on government were themselves of good enough character, once the reins of power are gathered in one place someone of bad character will soon recognize that they are there to be seized and exploited.

The appearance of alarmism is almost inescapable when such concerns are voiced about the possible future of America. But the apparent incongruity of these fears about the possible American future obtains precisely because we have the tradition of adamant limitations on government power, enforced by the vigorous exercise of ALL of those rights recognized in the Bill of Rights, and thus still enjoy the liberty that they defend. To voice fears about the rise of tyranny in places where such limitations have lapsed, or were never imposed in the first place, is merely to describe the past, present and future.

The erosion of liberty is typically prosecuted by the marginalization of, and then assault upon, its institutional and traditional bastions and their defenders-- one by one, with each next target falling faster than the last. The human dynamic which permits such efforts to succeed was poignantly expressed by Pastor Martin Niemöller, in words scratched on a wall in a Nazi death-camp. Read his words; consider the record; and then ask yourself: Is it really true that it can't happen here?

> *"First they came for the communists, and I did not speak out--*
>> *because I was not a communist;*
> *Then they came for the socialists, and I did not speak out--*
>> *because I was not a socialist;*
> *Then they came for the trade unionists, and I did not speak out--*
>> *because I was not a trade unionist;*
> *Then they came for the Jews, and I did not speak out--*
>> *because I was not a Jew;*
> *Then they came for me--*
>> *and there was no one left to speak out for me."*

Fiat Money, And The Formless Fed

᠌ᔓᏲᏲᏲ

In 1933, in the depths of the Great Depression, the United States government more-or-less defaulted on its debt. This was done in part by the adoption of House Joint Resolution 192 (along with subsequent related legislation):

JOINT RESOLUTION TO SUSPEND THE GOLD STANDARD AND ABROGATE THE GOLD CLAUSE, JUNE 5, 1933
H.J. Res. 192, 73rd Cong., 1st Session
Joint resolution to assure uniform value to the coins and currencies of the United States.
Whereas the holding of or dealing in gold affect the public interest, and are therefore subject to proper regulation and restriction; and
Whereas the existing emergency has disclosed that provisions of obligations which purport to give the obligee a right to require payment in gold or a particular kind of coin or currency of the United States, or in an amount of money of the United States measured thereby, obstruct the power of the Congress to regulate the value of money of the United States, and are inconsistent with the declared policy of the

Congress to maintain at all times the equal power of every dollar, coined or issued by the United States, in the markets and in the payment of debts.

Now, therefore, be it Resolved by the Senate and House of Representatives of the United States of America in Congress assembled, That

(a) every provision contained in or made with respect to any obligation which purports to give the obligee a right to require payment in gold or a particular kind of coin or currency, or in an amount in money of the United States measured thereby, is declared to be against Public Policy; and no such provision shall be contained in or made with respect to any obligation hereafter incurred. Every obligation, heretofore or hereafter incurred, whether or not any such provisions is contained therein or made with respect thereto, shall be discharged upon payment, dollar for dollar, in any such coin or currency which at the time of payment is legal tender for public and private debts. Any such provision contained in any law authorizing obligations to be issued by or under authority of the United States, is hereby repealed, but the repeal of any such provision shall not invalidate any other provision or authority contained in such law.

(b) As used in this resolution, the term "obligation" means an obligation (including every obligation of and to the United States, excepting currency) payable in money of the United States; and the term "coin or currency" means coin or currency of the United States, including Federal Reserve notes and circulating notes of Federal Reserve banks and national banking associations.

SEC. 2. The last sentence of paragraph (1) of subsection (b) of section 43 of the Act entitled " An Act to relieve the existing national economic emergency by increasing agricultural purchasing power, to raise revenue for extraordinary expenses incurred by reason of such emergency, to provide emergency relief with respect to agricultural indebtedness, to provide for the orderly liquidation of joint-stock land banks, and for other purposes", approved May 12, 1933, is amended to read as follows:

"All coins and currencies of the United States (including Federal Reserve notes and circulating notes of Federal Reserve banks and national banking associations) heretofore or hereafter coined or issued, shall be legal tender for all debts, public and private, public charges, taxes, duties, and dues, except that gold coins, when below the standard weight and limit of tolerance provided by law for the single piece, shall be legal tender only at valuation in proportion to their actual weight."

Approved June 5, 1933.

With this resolution, Congress purports to dictate to Americans that they must honor the paper 'nominal dollar' notes it prints at face value, making them 'dollars by decree', or 'fiat dollars'. (Genuine legal dollars are 371 4/16ths grains of pure silver.) Congress also uses this resolution to repudiate the federal government's obligation to redeem its outstanding debts as promised, aiming particularly at those of its securities which contained anti-inflationary clauses. Such clauses typically required that repayment of the loan be made in a fixed volume of gold directly, or that, if repaid with paper notes of any provenance, the nominal total value of such notes had to be adjusted such as to represent the purchasing power needed to buy the specified amount of gold at the time of repayment.

Gold clauses were included in contracts due to a recognition that the buying power of paper (nominal dollar) notes is inherently prone to fluctuation, and vulnerable to manipulation. The buying power of such notes is dependent on the accuracy-- and honesty-- of the issuing entity in confining the nominal aggregate value of all notes in circulation to the value of the real commodity(s) for which they can be redeemed. There is, after all, no inherent, natural limitation to that nominal aggregate value-- nothing but the restraint of the printer limits the number of nominal dollars in circulation.

To get a sense of this, imagine a laborer who trades a written promise to perform a day's work in the future for a payment today, having found a trading partner who needs no work done now, but knows that he will in the future (and perhaps sees a virtue in the liquidity of the note). This is fine so far, but what if the laborer issues these promises promiscuously, such that his outstanding obligations come to exceed his ability to redeem them all (either due to keeping poor records or in recognition of a lucrative, if dishonest, opportunity)? Obviously, the notes, sooner or later, correspondingly lose real value, both due to becoming more abundant relative to the other goods for which they are traded and because those to whom they are presented for trade become increasingly less confident that the notes will ever be redeemed at face value. All paper currency is subject to this risk, and the nominal dollar notes in circulation in America were, and are, no exception.

For example, during the first third of the twentieth century-- in which the United States established the Federal Reserve system and began an ongoing, increasingly promiscuous issue of notes-- nominal (that is, merely paper) United States dollars exhibited a decided fragility of value. For instance, a loan of 1000 nominal dollars made in 1900 which was paid back 33 years later in 1933 nominal dollars would be a repayment of considerably less value than had been lent: it actually took 1534 nominal dollars to buy as much in 1933 as the same number of dollars bought in 1900 as measured by the government's own Consumer Price Index-- a loss in purchasing power of 35%.

(I am providing figures based on the CPI because it is probably the most widely and easily understood yardstick. However, it is also the one which is least revealing of the overall corruption of the currency being measured, due to its incorporation of offsetting factors such as productivity gains and product quality improvements. The benefits reflected in such offsets (which will be discussed in detail later in this analysis) properly belong to the consumer whether his money has remained sound or not; and were that money to be sound, they would manifest as *increased* buying power under the CPI calculation. Calculated by a purer (if more difficult to consider) measure of the loss of buying power of a nominal dollar over the same period-- the 'unskilled labor rate'-- we find that by 1933 it took 2540 nominal dollars to equal the buying power of 1000 nominal dollars of 1900.)

Thus, gold clauses: Conscious of the unreliability of designated-nominal-value paper money, prudent lenders (or bond purchasers) would therefore specify that repayment of the loan was to be measured by stable buying power-- that is to say, the power to buy something, the inherent relative value of which was more-or-less unchanging. Gold, the time-tested standard of such stability, was the measuring stick of choice.

However, Congress, being disinclined to pay its debts in full measure, declared by means of HJR 192 that henceforth the government would make its payments with whatever it designated as 'currency' (in practice, Federal Reserve notes), in quantities sufficient to equal by *nominal* value what was specified in the agreement. The contract's *real* value specifications would be disregarded.

This was a change involving a great deal more than just the United States federal government stiffing its creditors. The means by which the repudiation of existing gold clauses was carried out involved the establishment of a new federal government currency regime-- a regime based upon federal reserve notes (FRNs). Unlike the immediately previous types of paper notes issued by the federal government, which were redeemable on demand in gold or silver and thus possessed the inherent value of the quantity of precious metal of which they signified ownership, the holder of an FRN has thereby an inherent claim on nothing more than the vague, variable-- and, in practice, constantly diminishing-- actual market value of the note. This is because FRNs are nothing but paper, and reflect ownership of nothing.

Further, the vague and variable market value of the notes is itself of a peculiar character. For one thing, while under the old regime the United States' creditors had been paid with real money, usable in any market in the world, under the new regime the instruments of payment can, for the most part, only be (legally) used as "currency" in America (or at varying rates of discount in other markets prepared to speculate as to their eventual purchasing power in America).

More significant is the underlying character of the notes as debt instruments. That is, the provisions of HJR 192 served to 'monetize' the federal debt-- issuing into circulation as "money" federal IOUs-- the sole definable utility of which is for the reciprocal payment of debts TO the federal government. In practice, this means that FRNs constitute "tax coupons", being legitimized against amounting to an ongoing 'check-kiting' scheme insofar as the nominal value emitted equals the total of all legitimate debts owed to the federal government in taxes.

Thus, HJR 192 gave birth to an intimate little cycle in which the government totals up what it calculates (or alleges) to be owing to it in taxes and uses this number to establish the volume of IOUs that it can issue. It then prints them up and pays them out to its creditors, who redeem them by spending them into the economy and buying real goods and services from the original tax-debtors on the basis of whose obligations the whole process began. We've all heard the assertion that, *"We owe the national debt to ourselves."* The 'monetization of debt' scheme constitutes the mechanism by which a fuzzy patina of legitimacy is lent to that entirely sophomoric and dissembling declaration.

In fact, we don't owe the national debt to ourselves, any more than Bob becomes legally obligated to the creditors of his buddy Sam once Sam loans him a fiver. The federal government owes the debt-- independently-- to individual Americans and others. However, Americans have long been encouraged to harbor a myth regarding the legal relationship between themselves and the federal government which provides 'intellectual' cover for the facile notion that, *"we owe the national debt to ourselves"*, and helps obscure the simple and obvious truth about who is a creditor of whom. This myth holds that 'we' (the American citizenry) *are* the federal government, *in a legal sense*. This myth was highly instrumental in making HJR 192 politically feasible (aided and abetted by the mind-numbing sense of crisis accompanying the Great Depression). It also serves to support much other bad governmental behavior. Thus, while HJR 192 and its peripheral effects could be usefully discussed at much greater length, it behooves us to turn our attention to the pernicious myth which facilitated that resolution's adoption-- and the broad truth against which that myth is deployed.

The Enemy Might Be Us, But The Government Isn't

As originally and properly established, the federal government constitutes an entity legally distinct from the population. It is, in this respect, an artificial person, generally characterized as a 'corporation'-- by which is meant not a business established by investment, etc., but rather a 'corporealization', or embodiment. This characterization is necessary to provide standing to the government-- in legal controversies, for example. Despite the affectation of the title 'The People' adopted by the state in such circumstances, clearly 'the people' can't sue-- or take any other adversarial position-- against one of the people, any more than you can sue yourself, or a part of yourself.

Indeed, virtually all functions and actions of the federal state require its corporeality in order to conform to the rule of law. The alternative is rule by mob and demagogue, and an essentially incoherent character of government-- incapable of being addressed, confronted, or restrained.

Consider this very fundamental example: the state's seeking of the material support of the people. Simply put, if the government is undistinguished from 'The People' (meaning the aggregate of the citizenry), then property in any individual citizen's possession would have to be considered as already-- and, impossibly, *also*-- in the possession of the government. By what principle could any spokesman for 'The People' argue that such property should be relocated, or disposed of according to the will of THAT member of 'The People' as opposed to the will of the member of 'The People' in whose possession it already is, and who created it in the first place? Under those circumstances, the controversy arising from the competing claims of right to the property is irresolvable (or at least, irresolvable in favor of whoever is alleging himself to represent 'The People') . Indeed, the basis for 'The People's' claim-- or even the legitimacy of whatever voice is presenting itself as 'the Voice of The People'-- could not be coherently articulated or defended.

Similarly, a mere aggregate of 'the people' cannot practically command, or even request, directed behavior by any one of the people. The targeted individual's own decisions are a part of those of 'the people's', and an attempt by others to override that individual's decisions could take no form but the action of a mob: no different than two neighbors conspiring to dictate to a third. Such an aggregate has no legitimate, distinct, and coherent voice or will. It is only when the theoretical aggregate is incorporated as a separate entity, and the many voices of its disparate parts are represented by the resulting single voice, that the will of one of the people can be meaningfully opposed by the aggregate of 'The People'. Only a distinct entity can have, or articulate, a legitimate (and judicially noticeable) claim in competition with another's.

We do, of course, sort out the issue of which voices will speak for 'The People' at any particular time. Unfortunately, the mechanism by which the aggregate of 'The People' is refined into that necessarily and legally distinct voice, will, and standing, under the American Constitutional system lends itself to confusion about the nature and legal ramifications of the distinction. Utilizing the mechanism of democratic process as it does, this Constitutional system makes very easy the inaccurate conflation of the aggregate with the distinct 'corporate person'. As it is (theoretically) the aggregate which picks those who speak and act for its corporate agent, we imagine (or are encouraged to imagine) that that agent remains undistinguished from the aggregate. But legally, this is simply and unambiguously not so. Once established, the 'corporate' embodiment that is the state is a distinct, separate artificial person viewed by the law as having its own purposes, rights, obligations, responsibilities and limitations. Other than to the degree that certain powers have been relinquished to it by their owners (on good behavior), the state is, under the law, indistinguishable from any other artificial person.

Bouvier's Dictionary of Law, Sixth Edition:
Corporation:

6. Nations or states, are denominated by publicists, bodies politic, and are said to have their affairs and interests, and to deliberate and resolve, in common. They thus become as moral persons, having an understanding and will peculiar to themselves, and are susceptible of obligations and laws. Vattel, 49. In this extensive sense the United States may be termed a corporation; and so may each state singly. Per Iredell, J. 3 Dall. 447.

The United States Supreme Court, US v. Perkins, 163 U.S. 625 (1896):

"...the United States are not one of the class of corporations intended by law to be exempt from taxation. What the corporations are to which the exemption was intended to apply are indicated by the tax laws of New York, and are confined to those of a religious, educational, charitable, or reformatory purpose. We think it was not intended to apply it to a purely political or governmental corporation, like the United States."

Under the law, while the sort of incoherent formlessness that is the nature of the un-incorporated state offers nothing capable of being bound down, it also offers nothing capable of exercising legitimate authority. As noted in our discussion above, it is the quality of being defined and distinct that clarifies what is otherwise one voice among many into that of the lawful government. Indeed, such definition and distinction is the whole point of the process of specifically identifying that one voice.

At bottom, the issue of corporeality as regards lawful government is a matter of first principles. After all, formlessness cannot secure the consent of the governed. One can only consent to a defined and knowable thing. Formlessness can only be acceded to by submission. So, the legitimate state cannot be formless, but must be defined-- and it is so defined by the powers delegated to it.

What can these powers be? Obviously, they can be no more than those possessed by the delegators themselves-- which is to say, no more than are possessed by human beings. Of great significance in this regard is the fact that the powers of human beings-- and thus those of any legitimate state-- are inherently limited by one factor beyond the purely physical: the responsibility which corresponds to every freedom of action. Willful actors are necessarily responsible actors, meaning that they are responsible-- as in, 'obliged to respond'-- to those who are directly affected by their actions. (The fine points of the nature of that responsibility, or the meaning of 'directly affected', are immaterial for purposes of this discussion-- it is enough to say that whatever relevant standards are applied to the delegators, the same must apply to their creation.) This inescapable responsibility is sometimes known as the moral dimension of freedom. It is what is meant by the reference of Supreme Court Justice Iredell, cited by Bouvier, to the government's becoming, through incorporation, "a moral person".

There is no mystical mechanism by which the fundamental aspect of responsibility can be stripped away in delegating authority to an agent, or state. One cannot authorize another to do what one otherwise may not do.

It has been suggested that we can, acting en masse, effectively accomplish an 'irresponsible authorization' by agreeing to hold our agent harmless in all that it does-- but this is an insupportable sophistry. First, such a notion is dependent upon an absolute and continuing universality of agreement-- a practical impossibility. Second, to so absolve another actor of unknown deeds lying in the future is simply another version of impermissible formlessness, to which consent cannot be given.

It has also been suggested that a middle ground exists: It is argued that the state has freedom of action without responsibility, but within certain limits which are flexible, or evolve-- and in any case must be discovered or endorsed by specialists or special processes, as the occasion demands. This, of course, is the impermissible formlessness again. It is just a version concealed behind a layer of intermediary (and beneficiary) actors; a version with, perhaps, a more torpid demeanor. Many varied attempts have been made over the millennia to dress up what amounts to a god-state, demanding submission rather than seeking consent from those upon whom it would act, in the clothing of legitimacy, through clever arguments. None can stand up to rational scrutiny, because the fundamental premise they seek to defend violates immutable natural law. Instead, that law requires, and America's founders respectfully conceived, a 'corporate' state having 'personhood' no different than that of any natural person in respect to its responsibility, or moral dimension.

Respect for this principle is, in fact, hardwired into the federal Constitution. A good example is the structure of federal taxation. Under this Constitutional regime, the firewall of apportionment-- complete with its restrictive legislative and administrative requirements-- is placed between the citizenry and any kind of direct tax, which is to say, taxes which otherwise would amount to a claim by decree-- as from an inchoate, or at least irresponsible, sovereign to a subordinate subject. In point of fact, Congress is only authorized to freely impose taxes on activities which are effectively connected with the government itself-- by virtue of which connection the government 'person' can claim its own naturally established right to a share in the proceeds.

It is clear, then, that the state is an independent actor, responsible for its own obligations and commitments, even when acting within its properly constituted limits. Nonetheless, there never has been, and never will be, an end to occasions in which the officers of the corporate state will seek to evade such responsibility by invoking the warm, fuzzy, all-one-big-family obscurity of formlessness, just as did Congress and the Roosevelt administration is 1933 by way of HJR 192. Thus, as has also been true since time immemorial, the responsibility for not being taken in by such nonsense falls to the rest of us.

Save The Children, Save The Future
ഇറ ൠ ൠ

As another September approaches, so too does another season of clamor regarding "values" in the nation's government schools. Sadly, all the effort and passion devoted to this debate will not only be completely ineffective at infusing the schools with virtuous character, it will actually be counterproductive, as it serves to divert the attention of parents and tax payers from clear thinking about the government education industry.

Parents who care about the culture in which their children are indoctrinated, or tax payers concerned about the kind of influences on future neighbors and voters for which they are paying should face the inconvenient truth that satisfactory respect for liberty and high cultural standards will never flourish, or even abide, in government schools. Not only are such schools inherently socialist, being founded, financed, and administered through socialist processes, they quite properly reject a formal adoption of or respect for any particular world view. They ARE coercively funded, and it would be utterly wrong for them to formally promote any particular creed, values, or perspective. As Thomas Jefferson said,

> *"To compel a man to furnish contributions of money for the propagation of opinions which he disbelieves and abhors, is sinful and tyrannical."*

Thus, such schools are incapable of offering an institutionally virtuous environment to which parents might commit a child. This would perhaps be acceptable by itself-- there are other forums in which virtue can be taught. But it is worse than simply that government schools cannot promote worthwhile values-- they of necessity promote destructive values. The problem is that they MUST promote some perspective, for an education of other than the narrowest scope cannot be "values neutral"

If an education was limited to math and the sciences, and even within that narrow range of subject matter was confined to only the numbers, values neutrality might be possible. But it is not possible under any circumstances to teach history, art, philosophy, literature, etc. objectively. All such material must be analyzed for causal relationships and interpreted as to meanings, and discriminatorily judged. Because this is so, and because the proper refusal of the schools to adopt any coherent, purposeful and time-tested perspective leaves a vacuum which must be filled, an inevitable proliferation of fads-- half-baked, contradictory, and self-serving-- and the mindless and nihilistic "values neutrality" of moral relativism and deconstructionism become the dominant cultural elements to which the students are exposed.

This corruptive process, natural in any institution not disciplined by a free market, has always been at play in the government schools. It is dramatically enhanced by court decisions bestowing on the pragmatic and socialist perspective the means to both impose itself and to suppress alternative influences. Every year that has passed since the government schools first became widespread in the early 20th century has seen an increasingly large and centralized bureaucracy grow more insular, alien, and less responsive to an increasingly captive "clientele", to whom every nickel of increased taxation extracted to support the government school is one less nickel available for buying an alternative private education.

The only productive response by parents and taxpayers to dissatisfaction or dismay with the government school cultural atmosphere is withdrawal. Withdrawal of children and withdrawal of support. To seek or endorse reform is to merely delay facing the truth, and in the meantime more irretrievable years of the children's lives are lost-- or worse. Here is another quote, which like the words of Thomas Jefferson cited earlier contains wisdom, but from the opposite end of the moral spectrum: V. I. Lenin, commenting with satisfaction on the performance of the government schools in the Soviet Union said,

> *"Give me a child for ten years, and I will give you a communist for life."*

The public school version of this is:

> *"Give me a child for twelve years, and I will give you an adult who is incapable of distinguishing right from wrong; certain that respect and reward are entitlements with no relationship to effort or accomplishment; a well-taught enemy of clarifying logic and intellectual rigor; and not only oblivious as to why any of these things are significant, but convinced that anyone not similarly handicapped is an enemy of social justice."*

While the refusal to pay the taxes extracted to finance government schools may not be practical (though they should be resisted and denounced with both words and votes), the refusal to surrender the children is certainly within the means and power of most two-parent households, as well as many single parents. In both situations, private schools offer fine alternatives to government schools at very reasonable prices, and the two-parent families have available the best possible educational approach: homeschooling. This alternative, rapidly gaining in popularity throughout all areas of the country and in all segments of society, offers unparalleled quality-of-life benefits as well as outstanding academic results, and for minimal costs of both money and time. It is viciously criticized by the government education establishment-- what more need be said to prove its worth?

Those voicing their concerns about the cultural morass into which the vast majority of the nation's children are thrown *do* have clear vision as to the gravity of the problem. There is no greater threat to the health and preservation of liberty and morality in America than these corrupt schools, churning out illiterate, cocky, ignorant socialists ready and waiting to vote and serve on juries-- along with an occasional literate and technically competent ethical void on the fast track to a career as a judge or politician. The education of our children is the future of America. In that regard, today's disgrace is tomorrow's catastrophe, and the magnitude of that catastrophe grows with each passing moment. Thus, patience with the niceties of debate or the political process is worse than simply time wasted, it is ground lost.

It's time to act, implementing some of the 'values' whose lack in the public schools trouble so many of us. Values such as taking individual responsibility for that future, and for the well-being of those children, even if the prospect sounds a little inconvenient or frightening. So, if you have school-age kids, look into homeschooling. Whether you have school-age kids or not, do everything possible to marginalize and defund government schools, in recognition of the fact that they are not simply not your friend-- they are your enemy. Each of us can be either the master of the future, or its victim. Master is better.

Bring 'Em Out Alive

The legal theories which keep the noxious abortion controversy alive in the face of steady majority opposition to the practice are really those of trespass and involuntary servitude, the Supreme Court's nonsense about a penumbra of privacy notwithstanding. There IS a penumbra of privacy in any system of government based on a limited delegation of authority to the state-- but it is irrelevant to the abortion question.

Citing that penumbra was an artifice by which the court tarted up with legalese the casting of the issue as a Hobson's choice between violating a defensible claim to autonomy by the woman on the one hand and the proactive death of the fetus on the other (with the ridiculous argument that early-stage humans are not 'human' being deployed like a thumb on one side of the scale). The strained privacy and fetal-inhumanity claims never commanded much meaningful respect from abortion's opponents; but instinctive American support for the much more defensible position regarding the woman's sovereignty furnished abortion advocates with a means to obscure the contrived and false characterization of the dilemma and steer consideration of the issue in a direction that favored their cause.

Revisiting that element reveals that a normal, well-established, and principled remedy for the conundrum was and is available-- the live, minimum-force-necessary eviction of the unwanted occupant/dependent. This remedy should be embraced as the morally superior, philosophically sound and politically feasible solution to the distasteful, but at least arguably legitimate, competition between the interests of certain people and their children. We can call it the "Bring 'Em Out Alive" compromise.

*****

The essential principles are simple: a woman can claim freedom from involuntarily providing a home and sustenance to the child, and can rightfully force it from her body; but when she does, it must be done without immediate harm to the child. This requirement of restraint is no different than that faced by an impatient and capable landowner, who must yet see even an innocent *uninvited* trespasser to the limits of her land alive, rather than save herself the walk by just gunning down the offender where he stands. The power to evict is unquestionable-- but so is the obligation to employ the minimum force necessary; and particularly where, as in the vast majority of abortions, the 'trespasser' is where he is due to the voluntary behavior of the now unwilling hostess.

Despite the obligation to see the baby safely out of herself and into the world, what would then become of it would not be the woman's business. Some might promptly die, some might more slowly do so; some, perhaps most or all, would become the immediate objects of rescue and preservation efforts by the rest of society. One thing is certain-- none of them would be in straits more dire than under the current regime.

As for the mothers, they would be modestly more inconvenienced than is the case for an abortion when the survival of the fetus is disregarded, but no more than would amount to a reasonable accommodation. Here, as in any other conventional trespass, there is a conflict of rights, but the balance of interests is simple and uncontroversial.

A greater inconvenience to those mothers than the lengthier, or more costly, or less available procedure would be filling out the forms waiving parental rights to the baby of which they are trying to be rid. I think that such a waiver would be a mandatory element of this compromise. It would be hard to argue with the proposition that such women are not fit parents, at least for these particular children.

This element, combined with what I think is the predictable behavior of the rest of society, would have its own beneficial effect on the entire issue. It is one thing to get your toenail clipped in the privacy of a supportive clinic which will go to any lengths to keep you from perceiving your condition as "being with child". It is quite another to sign the papers and then be operated on, understanding that an emergency medical team waits alongside you to scoop up your discarded baby and begin immediate heroic efforts to save or maintain its life so that it can go on to grow into a cherished little child in someone else's home, leaving your only relationship that of would-be killer and victim. I believe there would be few repeat customers.

*****

To "Bring 'Em Out Alive" would, I think, reveal the unnatural character of the abortive impulse so starkly as to stigmatize the practice severely, even while leaving it legal.

Though abortions would still be available to those who want them, such women would be marginalized into the ranks of drug-addicts, kleptomaniacs, and others characterized by a lack of self-discipline, personal integrity and sense of responsibility.

There will, therefore, be a great deal of resistance to this proposal among the extremists. They will cast about for arguments, and will chiefly flog the "not human/part of the mother (just a toenail)" proposition. Until now, the subtext of the previous debate has always tended to be, "Even if it is human, it's rights are trumped by the mother's (and besides, it's not human)". With the rights component removed, all that is left is the "not human/just a toenail" contention. (The health-of-the-mother argument has always rested on a comparison of the relative risks of abortion versus a full-term delivery. A live-baby abortion need be no more invasive or dangerous to the mother than a dead-baby abortion).

The most rudimentary analysis exposes this contention as nonsense: Once the genesis of the (genetically human) fetus is accomplished-- through the agency of two other (genetically independent) individuals-- its self-directed progress of development takes place whether the (genetically different) mother is present and providing the nurturing environment, or that environment is being provided by some guy in a lab coat with an incubator. What emerges from either protective environment is undeniably human. Thus the proposition that the fetus is not an individual human is absurd. Nonetheless, it will be fiercely advanced.

However, the large majority of even those who have previously ceded the debate to their fervent pro-abortion neighbors without much challenge will find it desirable to err on the side of caution and support this change. Indeed, already the recently revealed commonality of "botched" abortions resulting in babies unintentionally delivered alive and left in clinic closets or trash hampers to die has energized many previous fence-sitters to support stringent legislation regarding the care and treatment of those babies. An amazing transformation of the public perspective takes place when that "clipped toenail" becomes a live baby.

It will also be argued that some babies will suffer more under this solution-- dying slowly from exposure rather than quickly under the scalpel or vacuum device. But this false-- or at least, misdirected-- concern would rest on a failure to appreciate that the world is dynamic rather than static.

As mentioned earlier, much societal effort will turn toward rescue; more significantly, there would be many, many fewer abortions in the first place. Thus, in the worst case (the failure of society to mount the rescue campaign, or that effort's lack of comprehensive success), the same calculus by which we send our young men into battle would obtain, whereby a small number suffer hardship so that a greater number may be spared.

*****

In the end, to "Bring 'Em Out Alive" is a simple and principled solution to an otherwise intractable political problem, and it doesn't require a moral or legal perspective on the humanity of a fetus, or the propriety of abortion. A modest acknowledgement that uncertainty is reasonable will suffice, and, as we entertain no doubts regarding our own claim to the high status of human, self-respect alone demands no less of us.

Credit for the title 'Bring 'Em Out Alive' belongs to my estimable brother, Jack Reynold Hendrickson Jr., who coined it during the conversation in which this idea first saw the light of day.

The Criminal Rites Of Spring
ഇ൦൬ൾ൦ര

Over the next 3 1/2 months, thousands of American businesses and millions of individual citizens will use tax preparation specialists or software to help themselves commit one or more of a variety of serious crimes. Willfully, or, at best, negligently, these otherwise law-abiding Americans will prepare and execute a variety of fraudulent affidavits, resulting in serious harmful consequences for themselves and others. Despite being 100% personally responsible-- both morally and legally-- for its accuracy and its effects, these men and women will engage in a mass exercise of perjury, putting into the record sworn testimony about matters of which they are completely ignorant.

For instance, without ever having looked-- even for a moment-- at the highly specialized, quite-different-from-common-meaning statutory definitions of such custom legal terms as "employee", "trade or business", "employer" or "self-employed", these people will execute tax instruments declaring themselves to be one or more of these things. Those who do so inaccurately (the majority, I'm afraid) will at the same time subject themselves to a vastly higher tax liability than is legally appropriate; but whether right or wrong, each will swear to the truth and correctness of it all, to the best of their knowledge and belief.

Knowledge and belief. Read carefully now. The oath by which a tax instrument is executed doesn't say knowledge *or* belief, it says *knowledge and belief.* To make such an affirmation *without* any knowledge about what is being affirmed, and particularly without having made any effort to acquire such knowledge, is perjury-- a felony carrying a five year prison term. The criminal nature of the act is even independent of the accuracy or inaccuracy of what is being affirmed, just as would be your testifying to having seen the accused shoot the gun when you really didn't, the fact that he or she actually did notwithstanding.

Some might argue that they act in good faith, because they follow the instructions of others. They might say, for instance, that because they have been told to put the number found in box 1 of a W-2 onto line 7 of their 1040, they 'believe' that that number accurately reflects the *"wages as defined in 26 USC 3401(a) and/or 3121(a)"* they have received, for which that line on a 1040 is exclusively intended. I wouldn't buy it. I think the best that could credibly be claimed by that device is a belief as to what MUST be true, rather than what IS true. (Frankly, daring to speculate that precious few get out all their check stubs and add them up, I'd even go so far as to say that most couldn't honestly swear to a meaningful 'belief' that the *number* is correct, regardless of what it is supposed to represent.)

But it doesn't matter. Even if a 'belief' standard *allowed* for some latitude, mere 'belief' isn't good enough. Personal knowledge, as well as belief, is what is being attested to-- and what one has only been told by others in no way represents personal *knowledge.* Anyone who has not read the relevant law for himself or herself has no knowledge whether what has been put down on the form is right, or utterly wrong. This is true even of someone who DOES get out those paychecks and the adding machine, because each number on a tax return reflects two different kinds of testimony simultaneously: testimony as to an amount of something, and testimony as to the *legal nature* of that something. Swearing to the *'truth, completeness and correctness to the best of one's knowledge and belief'* of having received, for instance, $100 dollars of "wages" without knowing-- or making any effort to know-- the specialized legal definition of "wages", is a bald-faced lie.

*****

One thing that can be said about false testimony on a 1040 is that it only hurts the criminal, who typically ends up saddling himself or herself with a huge tax bite which is not otherwise owed. The other common tax-related felony which huge numbers across the country will commit between now and April 15th is of a much graver character. It involves false testimony regarding money paid to others, and makes victims of those others, as well as criminals of the testifiers themselves.

In some cases, this compound crime is committed through the issuing of W-2's-- affirmed under oath and attesting to the payment of "wages" as detailed earlier-- without any knowledge as to the truth or accuracy of the testimony. That represents perjury to start with, of course. However, as regards the overwhelming majority of Americans about whom these instruments will be executed, the assertion is also flat-out wrong. Nonetheless (and, in fact, quite deliberately), it will be relied upon by a hungry government to presume a tax liability on the part of the identified 'payee'. While common private-sector earnings are not taxable, the highly specialized kind of earnings which are assigned the title "wages" within the tax law definitely are. So, once the testimony on a W-2 has been entered into the record-- even if in complete ignorance (or disregard) of its import-- it becomes a body of evidence with which the payee must contend in doing his or her own tax filings. When that evidence is incorrect, dealing with it can be an enormous burden to that person.

In other cases, the compound 'information return' crime is committed with 1099's. Here, companies allege that payments made to others were in connection with a "trade or business", without the least notion of the narrow and specialized legal meaning of that phrase. To the degree that this is done in willful or negligent ignorance, this also amounts to perjury, because 1099's are transmitted over a sworn statement as to their accuracy (on Form 1096), just as are W-2's (by way of Form W-3). More importantly, a 1099, like a W-2, creates a burden of false evidence against the payee with which he or she will be obliged to deal-- sometimes at considerable trouble and expense. These are both truly despicable offenses.

(It is worth noting that the creation of W-2's and 1099's also establishes the basis for presumptions about the tax liability of the creating entity, often wrong and to its serious disfavor. Very considerable statutory civil penalties apply to the creation of erroneous information returns, as well. Still, as in the case of a errant 1040, no one but the filer is directly harmed by these effects.)

*****

It will come as a surprise to none but the most naive that the Internal Revenue Service-- the primary function of which is maximizing the amount of wealth turned over to the government-- will decline to recommend prosecution of the millions of felons committing the crimes outlined above. In fact, it won't even bring the crimes to the perp's attention, something which would clearly amount to a public service, but which would as clearly be contrary to that primary function. Rather, the 'service' will confine the bulk of its punitive efforts to harassing those about whom 'information returns' have been issued which have neither been acknowledged nor rebutted-- thus leaving an unresolved presumption of liability on the books.

It would be nice to think that those committing these crimes would police themselves, once made aware of the true nature of their unethical and unlawful behavior-- and many will. Others though, will balk and seek to excuse themselves from taking responsibility, saying, *"I don't want to be a criminal, but you say I have to testify based on my own knowledge. The federal revenue law, even condensed into the Internal Revenue Code, amounts to 3,413,780 words, plus regulations! Who can know the truth?"*

To that I shrug, and ask, *"How then can you sign a tax document?"* Perhaps you should not.

Perhaps you should take your records to your local IRS office and sit down with an agent and ask him or her to fill out and sign a return for you. Have them do the same with those W-2 and 1099 transmittals...

They won't, of course. However much the government likes to promote the myth that everything everyone earns in America is subject to the income tax, those who administer the system know perfectly well that this is nonsense. YOU can declare the money you received (or paid) to be "wages", or connected with a "trade or business"-- and once you sign on the dotted line the system will happily take you at your word. But unless the government is the one paying you, and thus can attest to its OWN *knowledge and belief* regarding your money, it has no legal basis to make any unilateral assertions of any kind about your earnings. Its agents certainly can't-- and won't-- sign anything under penalty of perjury which independently declares the legal status of payments made to you, or by you. (Neither will any of those 'professionals' who urge you to just do what the IRS wants, for that matter.) The fact is, calling upon the IRS (or anyone else) to relieve you of your responsibility would be fruitless-- getting you nothing but threats and curses.

What you *really* should do is read 'Cracking the Code-The Fascinating Truth About Taxation In America', and learn what important and misleading custom legal terms-- such as "wages", "employee", "employer", "trade or business", "self-employed", and others-- actually mean within the law. You should read 'Cracking the Code-...' and learn to whom the federal revenue laws apply; how those to whom they don't are made to think the contrary; and what the law provides for those who are being improperly treated.

You should read 'Cracking the Code-...' and equip yourself to sign your own future tax documents with confidence and a clear conscience (or confidently decline to create any in the first place); and to deal with erroneous evidence created about you by others who do not know, or respect, the truth. 3 1/2 days of reading 'Cracking the Code- The Fascinating Truth About Taxation In America' will make that 3 1/2 months between now and April 15th take on a whole new character.

So curl up in front of the fire with a good book; turn over a new leaf; and put your criminal past behind you. You'll be glad you did, and *that's* the truth.

The Full-Disservice Treatment
ༀ ☯ ༀ

Well, *both* autumn colors are now (or will soon be) decorating the landscape as the ubiquitous orange constriction zone barrels are joined once again by their more mobile cousins, the rolling yellow obstructions known as school buses. The bumblebee-like movement of the buses, restlessly rumbling from one brief stopping place to another-- if not quite in defiance of the laws of physics, certainly in defiance of the laws of traffic efficiency-- differs considerably from the inscrutable habits of the diminutive but more numerous barrel branch of the family, which will lie about in enormous herds in a state of absolute torpor, oblivious to all external conditions until, motivated by some stimulus as yet beyond the understanding of science, they rise as one in the dead of night and move en masse to a new grazing? communing? meditating? spot.

Nonetheless, the two seemingly disparate lifeforms are of a kind-- both symbiotic partners of larger organisms evolved over the course of decades to share in blood-meals sucked from the veins of tax payers. However, while the orange barrels and their partner/host road construction industry are merely the unavoidable byproduct of a more-or-less universally beneficial good, the school buses serve narrow private interests-- those of the public education industry and its clients-- and represent two direct subsidies by which important (and in the one case, subtle) costs are transferred from those clients to the rest of us in order to keep the marginal price of an inferior education product from pushing a dangerous portion of those clients and their political support over the departure threshold.

Schoolbuses have increasingly been transformed from a simple transportation utility into components of a full-service babysitting product as the decline of the schools from more-or-less sincerely intended educational institutions down to combination academic day-care center/social engineering factories has proceeded. They are relied upon to help offset the moral price of the years lost to the child with the benefit of convenience to the parents.

The welfare school industry, despite having firmly fastened itself upon the body-politic long ago, is increasingly dependent upon such transformational and value-added peripherals as its nominal justification becomes more and more obviously dysfunctional and counter-productive and its client base less stable. We've all seen what can happen: When another type of welfare was reformed recently with the addition of work requirements tied to the benefits, a very large portion of the users decided the pelf wasn't worth the effort and left the system, seriously threatening the justification of thousands of industry jobs. Many parents, presented with the prospect of not only yielding their child up to a lousy education but having to inconvenience themselves in the delivery of the victim as well, would crumble off the plantation at the margin.

Let's face it, the vast majority of public schools are held to the most insignificant standards, being measured academically merely on a relative basis and for the sake of appearances, and meaningfully assessed only insofar as they provide a reasonably safe storage place for the children of working parents. The constant shifting of the bar downwards puts the lie to any academic pretensions: the lowering of the

SAT standards, both a few years ago with an automatic addition to all scores of 100 unearned points, and then lately with the simplification of the test questions; "social promotion" right up to and including graduation (and the consequent dilution of course-work so that socially promoted students aren't made to suffer low self-esteem during classes in which they wouldn't belong if curriculum standards were maintained); "remedial" courses in colleges and universities across the country-- indeed, a college education has become what once was a high-school education, just too late to be as well absorbed, and cluttered with the distractions of the behaviors and license attendant upon young adulthood.

The Mackinac Center for Public Policy just released a study revealing that even within the context of today's grossly lower standards fully a third of graduating high school seniors in the state of Michigan lack basic skills in math, reading and writing. And remember, that's 1/3 of the *graduates*. While it appears virtually impossible to acquire accurate statewide numbers due to shameless book-cooking, Detroit's last reliable published graduation rate of 29.7% for far-and-away the largest single district in the state (some smaller districts have even lower rates) plus a national average 74% for the rest of the state suggests that it is likely that no more than ½ of the 18-year-olds processed through the public schools achieve even shaky skills in core subjects. Other states are likely to be little different.

Contrast that with the competition. The nascent home-schooling community is just a few years old, has only a rudimentary infrastructure of curricular materials and cultural resources, and is staffed by non-specialists who fit daily instruction in along with all the other responsibilities of homemaking and child-rearing-- frequently including the simultaneous management of disparately aged students following completely different lesson plans. Nonetheless, home schools are already outperforming the best of the 100+ year-old public school systems despite such system's huge expenditures under optimal conditions of specialization and support. Even private religious schools, asking tuition of just a fraction of the public school spending per pupil are uniformly recognized as providing a much superior product on virtually every front, and often despite devoting some portion of the schoolday (often a significant portion) to sectarian material.

So, the public school industry peddles convenience, safety, enrichment, and the socialization of Club Ed,-- *If you're not there, you're square! (The motto used to be, "If you're not here, you're queer", but they decided to drop that one a few years ago as not making sense anymore).*

And they come through:

- They'll pick your kids up more-or-less at the curb, amuse them all day long, equip Mom and Dad with plenty of 'round-the-water-cooler grist about "new" math and "whole language arts", and send home plenty of "A"s and not too much homework.

- They'll teach Johnny and Janey that an answer that's close is as good as one that's right; that cheating pays; and that everyone is entitled to self-respect just for showing up.

- They'll periodically explore your child's orifices, and periodically explain to him or her how to explore the orifices of other children.

- They'll have school plays, and field-trips, and cops in the hallways; and they'll teach your child to be politically active-- chiefly by sending them home with flyers urging "yes" votes on the latest school millage increase, and occasionally by busing them to the state capital to be exploited in a photo-op for some liberal cause.

- They'll give you school concerts to attend; sporting events to cheer at; and annual get-ready-for-school shopping events during which you can get in a little quality time.

- They'll teach your child to worship the Earth Mother and they'll send him or her to the Gay, Lesbian, Transgendered and Bisexual Community Resource Center (conveniently located next to the school nurse's office), for lectures on how to think correctly.

- They'll introduce your child to a library in which no copy of "Huckleberry Finn" will be found but where "Heather Has Two Mommies" will, and which still has 14 copies of "I, Rigoberto Menchu".

- They'll condition your child to perceive the State as the giver of wisdom, morality, and law.

- They'll deliver your kids as lifelong customers to whichever soft-drink company won the dispensing machine bid-- and give the advertisers on Channel One a pretty good shot at them as well.

- When all that is over, if you're not ready to put up with the little darlings yet, the school will store them in latch-key until you are.

They really are trying to be full-service crèches.

Considering the scope of this dedicated and generally harmful effort to add value, focusing on buses for comment may seem a bit off-target. But despite its stature as a Norman Rockwell cultural icon the prosaic schoolbus invites, even demands criticism as the most visible, most audacious interface between the welfare education industry and those of us not directly subjecting our children to its ministrations. Every workday morning, from September through June, nearly all of us on our way to a hard day earning the money taken from us for the support of the welfare schools will face extra time lost due to being subordinated to those bright yellow schoolbuses during our commute. Not only are our pockets picked to pay for the education of other people's kids, but we have to be inconvenienced on a daily basis to boot.

Imagine that along with a monthly food-stamp allotment came a card authorizing the beneficiary to cut in at the head of the checkout line in any grocery store. That would last about as long as it took voters to get their congressperson on the phone. Imagine if such a policy were being relied upon, or at least serving, as a perk to help keep food-stamp recipients from abandoning the program and providing for their own needs at their own expense. Such a thing would be indefensible. But that's just the role that schoolbuses fill. Much of the rest of what our taxes are spent on in the public schools do the same, but without the in-your-face, added-cost manner.

The extra time the rest of us spend stuck behind these free rides for the neighbor's kids is time denied to our own families. It's more than enough that we're paying for the product from which they're benefiting. They should handle the shipping themselves.

A Timely Reminder
ဆာၤသသ

The Ninth circuit panel got exactly one thing right in its ridiculous 2002 ruling regarding the Pledge of Allegiance (Newdow v. United States): that the "under God" phrase is the same (as far as Constitutional character is concerned) as "under no God". Both are expressions addressing the status of mankind and, though opposite sides, are of the same coin. In the very same breath the judges exercised their general sloppiness with references to Jesus and Zeus and Vishnu-- particular Gods, and therefore distinct from the class to which "under God" and "under no God" belong-- surprising no one who follows the antics of this most-frequently-reversed appellate court. In fact, this court so routinely plumbs the depths of socialist theory for nuggets of nonsense in service of a stubborn Marxism that only lazy journalism would cause a commentator to dwell on the subject, though many can't resist.

However, even those commentators eschewing the easy target on this story are generally missing, as did the court, the real issue here, which has nothing whatever to do with religion. Frankly, if the issue was religious, the Ninth would deserve more sober attention to its reasoning, for on the face of it, at least, they would be right. After all, no one should have to tolerate their money or their child being sent-- through actually and/or practically coercive means-- to an institution deliberately established to convey an understanding of reality which chooses one with which they disagree. *(When is someone going to step up to the plate here and get the Ninth to ban socialism from the schools for the same reasons?)*

But the real issue here is not religious, it is political, in the broad and fundamental sense of the word. If there is a God, then it is from that source that unalienable human rights-- which adhere to us simply for being human, which are not dependent upon or reducible by human art, and which predate and supercede all acts of man-- come. If not, then the virtues and benefits of being human depend for their character and defensibility on the craft of the ethicist or logician, are prey to the Big Lie and the demagogue, can be reasoned away with sweet practicalities and expediencies, or may be lost to short memories and ignorance.

"Endowed by their Creator with certain unalienable Rights..." goes the declaration, not "Agreed to by all right-thinking men as having unalienable rights", or "Determined by the best available science to be entitled to unalienable rights", or "Granted unalienable rights by their benevolent and representative government". In the politically pertinent sense, "Under God" means that the unalienable sovereignty which is the birthright of all humans and from which all other legitimate power to affect human liberty flows, comes first-- and is outside the reach of human interference, manipulation, or approval. As such, "Under God" invokes an infinitely potent counterbalance of authority to the otherwise dangerously overwhelming aura of authority and righteousness that an omnipresent and overweening state can and will bring to bear upon the subjects of its attention.

I have no quarrel with the view, which I suspect is correct, that those who added the phrase "under God" to the Pledge in 1954 meant no more by it than a simple sectarian exercise of power and piety, if not defiance. But in so doing they were unknowingly invoking the political principles to which I have referred. Thomas Jefferson said, *"Resistance to tyrants is obedience to God"*, meaning that only God has the authority to rule men without their consent, and any other who presumes to do so is illegitimate and a right object of overthrow and destruction. This was not an expression of piety, it was an expression of sovereignty, and of hierarchy.

The Founders frequently observed that the success of the American project depends upon a virtuous and religiously conscious citizenry, but not because of any superstitious expectations that God would smite the enemies of his pious servants, or visit upon an irreverent America the ten plagues of Egypt. These men were, for the most part, "Deists"-- acknowledging God as the divine Prime Mover, and the righteous object of man's reverence, gratitude and hope for redemption and ultimate reward, while rejecting the notion of an activist God who might interfere with free will and the earthly consequences of human behavior. God, to them, had his place in the day-to-day affairs of mortal humanity (outside the areas of psychology and spirituality) through preeminence in the political continuum.

In fact, the time of the American revolution was one of general religious liberalism, characterized by a throwing off of rigid and dogmatic doctrines like the near theocratically predisposed Calvinists and Puritans; the period was crowned the Age of Reason, and the Enlightenment. But even while the Founders asserted the power and right of the human mind to conceive and erect governments, a key part of their astonishing exercise of that power was recognition that by virtue of his equally divine origin even the rudest and meanest vagabond is secured the same rights as a Senator or President.

Relatedly, it is no mere coincidence that socialism, and other "-isms" which celebrate the State and deny the individual sovereignty of the people, despise, fear and seek to do away with religious consciousness. The intellectual servants of all such exploitations and tyrannies have confidence in their power to control or dominate a hierarchy determined solely by reason. They are conscious of possessing a competitive edge in such determinations, due to their willingness to lie, obfuscate, and, if need be, seduce-- through fear or reward-- the support of enough raw numbers to win any political contest in which the only factors are earthly and mortal. The concept of divine origin is a fatal stumbling block to their ambitions.

Their goal-- to subordinate, by principle, the individual to the State-- is thwarted when it is understood that man comes from God and the State comes from man. Without God in the equation the State can claim its rule to be the natural order of things, a righteous dispensation from Reason, as the divinely righteous Kings of earlier tyrannies who, having imposed themselves by the sword interposed themselves hierarchically between God and the People by claimed self-evident favored status to their own persons. The artificial State cannot claim such personal favor-- in fact, it must stand below the citizen when God stands above them both. But if God is not in the equation an individual man has only the rights and legitimacy accorded him by his fellows, and can 'reasonably' be held subordinate to their superior number, and the institutions that they ordain.

*****

The Supreme Court will doubtless overrule the foolish Ninth circuit (if its own inevitable en banc review doesn't do so first), but almost certainly using reasons as wrong as those it sets aside. Our national habit, after all, has become political expediency rather than political principle; thus do we sow the wind.

Good may yet come of this however, for perhaps some Americans will find in the occasion of this controversy (so providently coincidental with the anniversary of Independence Day) cause to reflect upon our heritage and its origins. The thoughts of one well-known writer might help set the course for such ruminations:

"Where the spirit of the Lord is, there is Liberty".
The Bible, II Corinthians 3:17.

"It is not the function of our government to keep the citizen from falling into error; it is the function of the citizen to keep the government from falling into error."
-Robert H. Jackson

Stop This Train
ဩအ္ဌဩ

"Every reform is only a mask under cover of which a more terrible reform, which dares not yet name itself, advances."
-R. W. Emerson

I participated in a gathering the other day which was addressed by the "Southeast Michigan Liaison" to Michigan's Secretary of State, Terry Lynn Land. This fellow was there on the Secretary's behalf, seeking to gain our support for her proposal to combine two impending expansions of federal control over Americans into one.

Ms. Land is proposing that the provisions of the Western Hemisphere Travel Initiative (WHTI)-- purporting to require that Americans produce a passport in order to gain re-entry into their own country-- be blended with those of the Real ID Act, which purport to require that Americans carry internal passports in order to enjoy the services of their own federal government and any institution or industry-- public or private-- which the feds have persuaded to accept subsidies from the public purse, or over which the federal government has assumed regulatory authority. Her proposal is that the new Real ID-qualified driver's licenses be "enhanced" with the data requirements mandated for external passports under the WHTI, so that the one set of papers serves both purposes.

Land reasons that her idea is just a matter of looking out for the interests of Michiganians. Since many of us travel in and out of Canada, many of us would be put to the trouble and expense of obtaining passports for the first time in their lives under the new protocol as it stands at present, since over all of the eighty years or so that modern American passports have been in use, these permission-slips have not been demanded for travel between the two countries. By making the internal passport serve as an external passport, we will be spared that trouble and expense.

Land is asking the Department of Homeland Security for approval to institute her notion on a pilot basis, and in advance of the 2008 Real ID deadline. She suggests that if it proves functional (how could it not?), the driver's licenses of all of the states would be similarly enhanced for the same purpose, and this latest transfer of power and authority from individual Americans to the central government could be accomplished with that much less trouble and fuss.

Hannah Arendt famously remarked on the banality of evil as manifested in Nazi Germany. She was referring to the contributions of those Germans who blithely incorporated the new regime's programs into their daily routine-- doing their best to see to it, for instance, that the trains kept running on time, despite the new cargo being transported. Think of what it might have meant to the history of the twentieth century if the average German had taken a philosophical view, rather than a pragmatic one, and had put down his or her tools and said, "No!" Land should do just that, rather than seek to make the adoption of these schemes more palatable.

I am not suggesting that the ambitions behind the WHTI and the Real ID Act are to be classed with those of Nazism. But I am stating outright that even though the true character of those ambitions are not known to me, they are wrong and bad, and should be resisted, not enabled.

For instance, when the concept of the Real ID Act is given a little thought, it becomes clear that whatever purpose will be served by it, it will be no good purpose. After all, it would be ridiculous to suggest that the implementation of an internal passport will eliminate-- or even mitigate-- any danger from "terrorism" (such as there is...). Are we to imagine that this program will lead to the removal of metal detectors at federal courthouses, and searches at airports, etc.? Of course not.

The prospect that his or her identity will be definitively established before entering the target, either as an American citizen with a "Real ID", or as a foreign visitor with whatever alternative will inevitably and unavoidably by provided for, is NOT going to deter a suicide attacker, is it? Similarly, those who intend to smuggle explosives, or whatever, into a target will do so unhindered-- and walk out again-- if all that is done at the door is a check of his or her "Real ID".

As for the WHTI, virtually the same can be said. The dangers posed by terrorists are not due to their anonymity, and unless we intend to refuse entry to any non-Americans upon the adoption of WHTI-- and we do not-- it will be a meaningless imposition, as far as the prevention of terrorism is concerned. But it will not be a meaningless imposition in other respects: With the adoption of these policies Americans-- who once did not-- will now carry papers to show bureaucrats on demand, and as a consequence of which their movements will be trackable and recordable, and they will evermore be at the mercy of the competence, caprice, ire or ill purpose of those who control the database.

Furthermore, only a fool or a child would fail to recognize that though the current protocol only makes access to "federally connected" services, institutions and industries dependent on the possession of a properly-functioning "Real ID", it will only be the briefest of intervals before most of one's day-to-day affairs are similarly dependent.

Indeed, consider this: The vast majority of banks in America are federal instrumentalities, legally. Thus, even before it inevitably becomes the case that a "Real ID" in good standing is necessary to get phone service or groceries, the status of one's 'papers' will determine not only whether or not one can board an airplane, but also whether or not access to one's money is permitted.

Rather than seeking ways to ease Michigan into participation with this noxious scheme with the least amount of friction, Terry Lynn Land (and every other Secretary of State) should be figuring out how to make this train-ride as bumpy as possible, in an effort to foment a statewide refusal to participate. Personally, I can't think of a single federal "service" I couldn't live without (or to which Michigan couldn't furnish a perfectly acceptable alternative); and if the 10 million citizens of Michigan (or any other state) were to say "No, thanks," to this scheme, I'm confident that Congress would quickly come up with a more palatable alternative.

Things Are Not As Bad As You Might Be Thinking
ഉ෬෬෬

This has to be an interesting time for those who insist that every federal legislative declaration has more-or-less universal application throughout America. We are now within the time period during which effective political speech is prohibited within the jurisdiction of the Bipartisan Campaign Finance Reform Act. Thus, those of the aforementioned persuasion must now be acutely suffering under the conviction that the United States Constitution, and the unique political heritage that it reflects, has been stolen away from them and their children by an open conspiracy of Congress, the Executive, and the Supreme Court.

There is, after all, no other conclusion possible to those within this group. The very first clause in the Bill of Rights says, unambiguously and with no exceptions provided, that "Congress shall make no law... ...abridging the freedom of speech...". If you believe that the federal election laws (of which the BCRA is a part) mandatorily apply to every American, then you believe that the First Amendment has been overthrown. (If you believe that language as clear as "Congress shall make no law... ...abridging the freedom of speech..." is open to 'interpretation', then you have embraced a level of sophistication so advanced as to amount to simple-mindedness. You may leave now--there's probably something you'd like on TV.)

Of course, federal legislative acts do NOT have such universal application. As the Supreme Court has helpfully observed,

> *"Words having universal scope, such as 'every contract in restraint of trade,' 'every person who shall monopolize,' etc., will be taken, as a matter of course, to mean only everyone subject to such legislation, not all that the legislator subsequently may be able to catch."* United States Supreme Court, American Banana Co. v. United Fruit Co., 213 U.S. 347 (1909).

Who IS *"subject to* [federal] *legislation"* was spelled out fairly crisply by the Eisenhower administration's Interdepartmental Committee for the Study of Jurisdiction Over Federal Areas within the States. The pertinent portion of its report points out that,

> *"It scarcely needs to be said that unless there has been a transfer of jurisdiction (1) pursuant to clause 17 by a Federal acquisition of land with State consent, or (2) by cession from the State to the Federal government, or unless the Federal Government has reserved jurisdiction upon the admission of the State, the Federal Government possesses no legislative jurisdiction over any area within a State, such jurisdiction being for exercise entirely by the States, subject to non-interference by the State with Federal functions, and subject to the free exercise by the Federal Government of rights with respect to the use, protection, and disposition of its property".*

In making its declaration, the commission merely acknowledged the Constitution's specifications, as expressed by

the Supreme Court in, for instance, New Orleans v. United
States, 35 U.S. (10 Pet.) 662, 737 (1836):

> "*Special provision is made in the Constitution for the
> cession of jurisdiction from the States over places where
> the federal government shall establish forts or other
> military works. And it is only in these places, or in the
> territories of the United States, where it can exercise a
> general jurisdiction.*"

...and the generally limited authority of the federal government,
as expressed by the high court in, as an example, one of my
personal favorites, Stanton v. Baltic Mining Co, 240 U.S. 103
(1916):

> "*Mark, of course, in saying this we are not here
> considering a tax... entirely beyond the scope of the
> taxing power of Congress, and where consequently no
> authority to impose a burden, either direct or indirect,
> exists.*"

(Now, admit it... How many of you believed two minutes ago
that there WERE any limits to the authority of Congress to
impose a tax?)

I realize that the prospect of acknowledging the limits of
federal jurisdiction is highly disturbing. It represents an
"everything you know is wrong" kind of paradigm-shift.

Of course, it also represents a key to understanding all
those hundreds (or thousands) of legislative enactments that
have always appeared to contradict everything you thought you
knew about the American governmental structure. That's
actually a pretty bright silver lining mitigating the dark cloud of
having the scales fall from your eyes, no? Think of the liberty
suddenly restored to you by simply recognizing that darn near
every cheap political payoff to some loudmouthed constituent
group issued by Congress over the last 100 years or so has just
been a snow-job, incorporating high-falutin' rhetoric into laws
having actual force only within the small amount of territory

subject to general federal jurisdictional control under the Constitution, and the handful of tiny areas ceded by the states.

Congress has gotten pretty bold at this game over the years. Back in the 1960's when the 'Fair Housing Act' was passed, for instance, Congress was honest enough to acknowledge its jurisdictional limitations, pointedly stating that,

> *"It is the policy of the United States to provide, **within constitutional limitations**, for fair housing throughout the United States"* (emphasis added).

These days such courtesies are largely abandoned. Taking full advantage of the fact that it is solely the responsibility of other interested parties to know or learn the limitations to which a statute is jurisdictionally confined, today Congress routinely passes laws and resolutions, and authorizes or endorses executive orders, which are, on their faces, of the most dictatorial and far-reaching character-- leaving it up to you and me to recognize that none of them have the least authority over private, union-state Americans. Such pronouncements might be like Royal Decrees to clerks in the Rayburn building or a citizen of Guam, but they're just hot air and political posturing to a guy from Akron (unless the guy from Akron doesn't know the rules of the game, of course).

Of course, I could be wrong, and we could simply be in the grip of a tyranny distinguished from other historical examples solely by its deployment of fanciful legislative fig-leaves to paper over an otherwise naked exercise of illegitimate power. But then I'd have to be having this smuggled to you in your guerilla camp in the hills, right? Certainly I would, because there's no way you would abide the obvious subversion of your Constitution, and if I AM wrong, that's exactly what laws like the Bipartisan Campaign Reform Act represent.

Happily, I'm not wrong, and taking up arms is unnecessary, so far. Still, there ARE battles to be fought, in courtrooms and schoolrooms. Silenced is silenced, whether because a gag is stuffed into your mouth by a jack-booted thug, or because you are simply frightened or fooled into keeping your lips sealed on your own.

Furthermore, ruling, and obedience, become hard habits to break when practiced for too long; and a compliant and deluded master will soon change places with an ambitious and conniving servant. So praise the Lord and pass the law books; and be happy the reality is what it is. The alternative-- sooner or later, but sure as the sun coming up in the morning-- is a bloody horror.

Getting Education Reform Right

ഇൗ Ⳝ⳺ ⳺Ⳳ

As the pressure mounts nationwide to address the catastrophe of the welfare (public) school system, much attention is being paid to various forms of the 'Tuition Tax Credit'. A number of states have adopted one or another version, which typically provide a credit against state taxes for parents taking care of their children's educational needs outside of the welfare schools, and sometimes for *anyone* taking care of *any* child's educational expenses, including through philanthropy toward children not related to the benefactor. Some versions even make the credit 'refundable' (which is to say, a voucher).

These legislative efforts are admirable for acknowledging the desperate need for reform; most of them (the voucher style excepted) share the virtue of clarity regarding both the purpose and provenance of educational expenditures; but all of them are fatally flawed. The key to a successful reform is the elimination of state involvement-- be it direct or through tax policies spurring parents toward certain favored choices-- in education decision-making. The typical tuition tax credit plan, however, leaves the state fully in the driver's seat, by tying benefits to what will inevitably be a state-defined behavior.

The flaw lies in the references to "educational expenses" through which these plans both undermine their prime ideological virtue and make themselves vulnerable to subversion by the very interests against which they are ostensibly deployed. It is typical of reform plans arrayed against a host of entrenched and tax-fattened special interests to incorporate language making conceptual concessions to the status quo-- thus do they combat the reflexive rejection of change natural to the disinterested majority. Such concessions, though dismissed by their boosters as mere lip service, are often the slow-acting infections that not only gut the reforms but add to the cynicism and cognitive dissonance polluting relevant public policy, and so it is here.

The desperately important concern for the well-being of children animating the push for reform is responsive to a complex threat grounded in the *public oversight* of the education process as well as the sloth, incompetence and corruption inevitable in publicly financed schooling. The poor quality of academic instruction and (sometimes) physical danger are the most obvious and easily referenced failings of the public schools, and are acknowledged even by the parasites feeding from that particular trough-- both because they are undeniable and because plausible arguments can be made that they could (theoretically) be addressed by increased funding. But it is the hijacking of child-rearing authority realized through the indoctrination of the captive children that motivates the enthusiasm for reform of the vast majority of supportive parents.

Though punditry routinely cites the poverty-stricken ghetto resident as the constituency most interested in or able to benefit from freedom of choice in education, it is the parent sacrificing to keep their child in a private school, or joining the rapidly growing ranks of homeschoolers that represent the real, quantifiable constituency for reform. These predominately suburban and rural parents are not fleeing illiteracy or gang violence, they are escaping socialist indoctrination and the psychic rot of relativism, and the other related mental illnesses with which the public schools are infested. Such defective practices of thought are, of course, natural contributors to the coincident collapse of academic standards and discipline. After all, you can't preach socialism and teach sound economics or history; or worship relativism and demand meaningful standards of behavior and performance, at the same time.

Successful reform, in the minds of these parents, means mitigating the tax burden for services for their own children in which they have no interest and from which they receive no benefit, and securing to themselves complete control over the up-bringing of those children-- including any and all educational decisions regarding nature, content and venue. Thus, the references in tuition tax credit legislation to "educational expenses", which can be read, in anticipation of the inevitable judicial proceedings invited by such ambiguous language, as "qualifying educational expenses", or more bluntly as "approved educational expenses", must be excised; and the credit should be based simply on the relief to the public system provided by a parent through the withdrawal of a qualifying child from consuming its "benefits".

Parents who are being taxed less, or no more than, what is being publicly allocated for their child should be credited with all that they are paying. Parents being taxed for more than is being allocated for their child should be credited with that allocated amount, with the remainder continuing to provide welfare for other peoples children as it does now (until such time as the entire public education system can be shut down).

Resulting legislation would look something like this: *"Any parent who relieves the public of the expense of educating a child shall receive a tax credit for any and all amounts up to the total dollar value of such relief, which value shall equal the per pupil expenditure on education in the school district in which the child resides".* If a benefactor element is considered desirable, the word "person" would be put in place of "parent". The "refundable" versions should be called what they are, *welfare,* and left to their own legislative efforts under that category of public policy.

Though the commonly understood definition of tuition is "The charge or payment for instruction," the original meaning of the word is, "Guardianship; care". Its origin is the Latin word for guard: *Tuitio.* Thus, a 'Tuition Tax Credit' is really a 'Guardianship Tax Credit'. It is uniquely the role-- and right-- of parents to claim and exercise the guardianship of their children; though they may choose to entrust those treasures to the care of another, it is a temporary and revocable delegation. As with any other delegation, when it is dissolved, so too is the claim of the former trustee to compensation for the services rendered, be that trustee an individual, an institution, or a government.

The longer that education reform is delayed, the more desperately it is needed. So, let's do it, certainly. But let's do it right.

Strolling Down Memory Lane
෨෦෬෨෦෬

I sat down to write a piece on the 'Bipartisan Campaign Reform Act' today-- intending to fulminate a bit, discuss the proper and Constitutional limits of the federal government, and so forth. But just as I got started, I suddenly remembered that America has already gone down this very path once before, which occasion had prompted a couple of far finer commentaries on the subject than anything I could offer. I'm going to share those commentaries with you in lieu of my own remarks. *(What's that? Do I hear cheering?!!!)* The reader will be better served than otherwise, and I'll push the Carpal Tunnel Syndrome which doubtless lies in my future a little further off.

Here's the background: 206 years ago, like today, the offices of the United States government were controlled by people very acclimated and attuned to the prerogatives of aristocracy. In that earlier time the acclimation was not due to personal experience as such, but rather from having grown up seeing such prerogatives exercised by others with the sort of casual arrogance that comes from having been born to it; the attunement was due to the ageless corruption that a taste of power works upon all.

Today's Lord Wannabe's are attuned for the same reason as their forebears, but are acclimated by direct experience-- being the beneficiaries of the slavish adulation of their supporters; the fascination of the media to the point of minor-- or sometimes major-- stardom; a benevolent and reciprocal prosecutorial latitude (as long as they don't rock the boat too much); and a compensation, perks, benefits, and retirement package that would have been the envy of many a landed aristocrat in King George's court.

Then, as now, these divine-right-minded solons found themselves the occasional objects of criticism at the hands of the mere citizenry, and felt that they had no need to abide the indignity. Thus, as now, they outlawed it.

The act passed in 1798 which so closely anticipated today's BCRA was known as The Sedition Act, an amendment of a measure passed shortly before providing for the summary deportation of foreigners (in practice, only politically active foreigners), popularly referred to as The Alien Act. In pertinent part, the amendment made criminal the saying of nasty or unpleasant things about members of Congress or the administration.

To give this earlier law its due, it was less outrageous than the current version, in that it (theoretically) confined its attention to libels (although this made it redundant, and thus more-or-less transparently ill-intended), and provided for the truth of the nasty or unpleasant thing said as an affirmative defense in a prosecution, something conspicuously missing from the BCRA. Nonetheless, numerous prosecutions over things printed and said which were true took place under its auspices. The text of that pertinent part is as follows:

An Act in Addition to the Act Entitled "An Act for the Punishment of Certain Crimes Against the United States."

SEC. 2. And be it further enacted, That if any person shall write, print, utter or publish, or shall cause or procure to be written, printed, uttered or published, or shall knowingly and willingly assist or aid in writing, printing, uttering or publishing any false, scandalous and malicious writing or writings against the government of the United States, or either house of the Congress of the United States, or the President of the United States, with intent to defame the said government, or either house of the said Congress, or the said President, or to bring them, or either of them, into contempt or disrepute; or to excite against them, or either or any of them, the hatred of the good people of the United States, or to stir up sedition within the United States, or to excite any unlawful combinations therein, for opposing or resisting any law of the United States, or any act of the President of the United States, done in pursuance of any such law, or of the powers in him vested by the constitution of the United States, or to resist, oppose, or defeat any such law or act, or to aid, encourage or abet any hostile designs of any foreign nation against United States, their people or government, then such person, being thereof convicted before any court of the United States having jurisdiction thereof, shall be punished by a fine not exceeding two thousand dollars, and by imprisonment not exceeding two years.

SEC. 3. And be it further enacted and declared, That if any person shall be prosecuted under this act, for the writing or publishing any libel aforesaid, it shall be lawful for the defendant, upon the trial of the cause, to

give in evidence in his defence, the truth of the matter
contained in Republication charged as a libel. And the
jury who shall try the cause, shall have a right to
determine the law and the fact, under the direction of
the court, as in other cases.

[Editorial interruption: The reader is encouraged to take careful note of the language in that last sentence regarding the right of the jury to determine THE LAW as well as the fact, and to remember it the next time the opportunity for service in the high civic office of juror is afforded him or her. Ok, we now return to the regularly scheduled usurpation, which is already in progress...]

SEC. 4. And be it further enacted, That this act shall
continue and be in force until the third day of March,
one thousand eight hundred and one, and no longer:
Provided, that the expiration of the act shall not prevent
or defeat a prosecution and punishment of any offence
against the law, during the time it shall be in force.
APPROVED, July 14, 1798.

This is pretty tame stuff, compared to a direct abrogation of the right to say *anything* about an officeholder for months at a time, and particularly right before an election. Still, it was recognized as the slimy aspiration to tyranny that it was, and great minds and spirits rose to the occasion.

What follows are the expressions of two of those great minds and spirits: Thomas Jefferson, who gave voice to the righteous and united reaction of the people of Kentucky, and James Madison, who did the same for his fellow Virginians. They are long, but beautiful and rewarding.

We, for whom the corrupt defiance of the words and meaning of the Constitution against which they inveigh is now generations old, would do well to study closely the open-eyed regard of the threat to liberty-- and the narrow-eyed resoluteness in its defense-- revealed in these words:

The Kentucky Resolutions of 1798

1. Resolved, That the several States composing, the United States of America, are not united on the principle of unlimited submission to their general government; but that, by a compact under the style and title of a Constitution for the United States, and of amendments thereto, they constituted a general government for special purposes — delegated to that government certain definite powers, reserving, each State to itself, the residuary mass of right to their own self-government; and that whensoever the general government assumes undelegated powers, its acts are unauthoritative, void, and of no force: that to this compact each State acceded as a State, and is an integral part, its co-States forming, as to itself, the other party: that the government created by this compact was not made the exclusive or final judge of the extent of the powers delegated to itself; since that would have made its discretion, and not the Constitution, the measure of its powers; but that, as in all other cases of compact among powers having no common judge, each party has an equal right to judge for itself, as well of infractions as of the mode and measure of redress.

2. Resolved, That the Constitution of the United States, having delegated to Congress a power to punish treason, counterfeiting the securities and current coin of the United States, piracies, and felonies committed on the high seas, and offenses against the law of nations, and no other crimes, whatsoever; and it being true as a general principle, and one of the amendments to the Constitution having also declared, that "the powers not delegated to the United States by the Constitution, not prohibited by it to the States, are reserved to the States respectively, or to the people," therefore the act of Congress, passed on the 14th day of July, 1798, and intituled "An Act in addition to the act intituled An Act for the punishment of certain crimes against the United States," as also the act passed by them on the — day of June, 1798, intituled "An Act to punish frauds committed on the bank of the United States," (and all their other acts which assume to create, define, or punish crimes, other than those so enumerated in the Constitution,) are altogether void, and of no force; and that the power to create, define, and punish such other crimes is reserved, and, of right, appertains solely and exclusively to the respective States, each within its own territory.

3. Resolved, That it is true as a general principle, and is also expressly declared by one of the amendments to the Constitutions, that "the powers not delegated to the United States by the Constitution, our prohibited by it to the States, are reserved to the States respectively, or to the people"; and that no power over the freedom of religion, freedom of speech, or freedom of the press being delegated to the United States by the Constitution, nor prohibited by it to the States, all lawful powers respecting the same did of right remain, and were reserved to the States or the people: that thus was manifested their determination to retain to themselves the right of judging how far the licentiousness of speech and of the press may be abridged without lessening their useful freedom, and how far those abuses which cannot be separated from their use should be tolerated, rather than the use be destroyed. And thus also they guarded against all abridgment by the United States of the freedom of religious opinions and exercises, and retained to themselves the right of protecting the same, as this State, by a law passed on the general demand of its citizens, had already protected them from all human restraint or interference. And that in addition to this general principle and express declaration, another and more special provision has been made by one of the amendments to the Constitution, which expressly declares, that "Congress shall make no law respecting an establishment of religion, or prohibiting the free exercise thereof, or abridging the freedom of speech or of the press": thereby guarding in the same sentence, and under the same words, the freedom of religion, of speech, and of the press: insomuch, that whatever violated either, throws down the sanctuary which covers the others, and that libels, falsehood, and defamation, equally with heresy and false religion, are withheld from the cognizance of federal tribunals. That, therefore, the act of Congress of the United States, passed on the 14th day of July, 1798, intituled "An Act in addition to the act intituled An Act for the punishment of certain crimes against the United States," which does abridge the freedom of the press, is not law, but is altogether void, and of no force.

4. Resolved, That alien friends are under the jurisdiction and protection of the laws of the State wherein they are: that no power over them has been delegated to the United States, nor prohibited to the individual States, distinct from their power over citizens. And it being true as a general principle, and one of the amendments to the Constitution having also declared, that "the powers not delegated to the United States by the Constitution, nor prohibited by it to the States, are reserved to the States respectively, or to the people," the act of the Congress of the United States, passed on the — day of July, 1798, intituled "An Act concerning aliens," which assumes powers over alien friends, not delegated by the Constitution, is not law, but is altogether void, and of no force.

5. Resolved. That in addition to the general principle, as well as the express declaration, that powers not delegated are reserved, another and more special provision, inserted in the Constitution from abundant caution, has declared that "the migration or importation of such persons as any of the States now existing shall think proper to admit, shall not be prohibited by the Congress prior to the year 1808" that this commonwealth does admit the migration of alien friends, described as the subject of the said act concerning aliens: that a provision against prohibiting their migration, is a provision against all acts equivalent thereto, or it would be nugatory: that to remove them when migrated, is equivalent to a prohibition of their migration, and is, therefore, contrary to the said provision of the Constitution, and void.

6. Resolved, That the imprisonment of a person under the protection of the laws of this commonwealth, on his failure to obey the simple order of the President to depart out of the United States, as is undertaken by said act intituled "An Act concerning aliens" is contrary to the Constitution, one amendment to which has provided that "no person shalt be deprived of liberty without due progress of law"; and that another having provided that "in all criminal prosecutions the accused shall enjoy the right to public trial by an impartial jury, to be informed of the nature and cause of the accusation, to be confronted with the witnesses against him, to have compulsory process for obtaining witnesses in his favor, and to have the assistance of counsel for his defense;" the same act, undertaking to authorize the President to remove a person out of the United States, who is under the protection of the law, on his own suspicion, without accusation, without jury, without public trial, without confrontation of the witnesses against him, without hearing witnesses in his favor, without defense, without counsel, is contrary to the provision also of the Constitution, is therefore not law, but utterly void, and of no force: that transferring the power of judging any person, who is under the protection of the laws from the courts, to the President of the United States, as is undertaken by the same act concerning aliens, is against the article of the Constitution which provides that "the judicial power of the United States shall be vested in courts, the judges of which shall hold their offices during good behavior"; and that the said act is void for that reason also. And it is further to be noted, that this transfer of judiciary power is to that magistrate of the general government who already possesses all the Executive, and a negative on all Legislative powers.

7. Resolved, That the construction applied by the General Government (as is evidenced by sundry of their proceedings) to those parts of the Constitution of the United States which delegate to Congress a power "to lay and collect taxes, duties, imports, and excises, to pay the debts, and provide for the common defense and general welfare of the United States," and "to make all laws which shall be necessary and proper for carrying into execution, the powers vested by the Constitution in the government of the United States, or in any department or officer thereof," goes to the destruction of all limits prescribed to their powers by the Constitution: that words meant by the instrument to be subsidiary only to the execution of limited powers, ought not to be so construed as themselves to give unlimited powers, nor a part to be so taken as to destroy the whole residue of that instrument: that the proceedings of the General Government under color of these articles, will be a fit and necessary subject of revisal and correction, at a time of greater tranquillity, while those specified in the preceding resolutions call for immediate redress.

8th. Resolved, That a committee of conference and correspondence be appointed, who shall have in charge to communicate the preceding resolutions to the Legislatures of the several States: to assure them that this commonwealth continues in the same esteem of their friendship and union which it has manifested from that moment at which a common danger first suggested a common union: that it considers union, for specified national purposes, and particularly to those *specified in their late federal compact, to be friendly, to the peace, happiness and prosperity of all the States: that faithful to that compact, according to the plain intent and meaning in which it was understood and acceded to by the several parties, it is sincerely anxious for its preservation: that it does also believe, that to take from the States all the powers of self-government and transfer them to a general and consolidated government, without regard to the special delegations and reservations solemnly agreed to in that compact, is not for the peace, happiness or prosperity of these States; and that therefore this commonwealth is determined, as it doubts not its co-States are, to submit to undelegated, and consequently unlimited powers in no man, or body of men on earth: that in cases of an abuse of the delegated powers, the members of the general government, being chosen by the people, a change by the people would be the constitutional remedy; but, where powers are assumed which have not been delegated, a nullification of the act is the rightful remedy: that every State has a natural right in cases not within the compact, (casus non fœderis) to nullify of their own authority all assumptions of power by others within their limits: that without this right, they would be under the dominion, absolute and unlimited, of whosoever might exercise this right of judgment for them: that nevertheless, this commonwealth, from motives of regard and respect for its co States, has wished to communicate with them on the subject: that with them alone it is proper to communicate, they alone being parties to the compact, and solely authorized to judge in the last resort of the powers exercised under it, Congress being not a party, but merely the creature of the compact, and subject as to its assumptions of power to the final judgment of those by whom, and for whose use itself and its powers were all created and modified: that if the acts before specified should stand, these conclusions would flow from them; that the general government may place any act they think proper on the list of crimes and punish it themselves whether enumerated or not enumerated by the constitution as cognizable by them: that they may transfer its cognizance to the President, or any other person, who may himself be the accuser, counsel, judge and jury, whose suspicions may be the evidence, his order the sentence, his officer the executioner, and his breast the sole record of the transaction: that a very numerous and valuable description of the inhabitants of these States being, by this precedent, reduced, as outlaws, to the absolute dominion of one man, and the barrier of the Constitution thus swept away from us all, no rampart now remains against the passions and the powers of a majority in Congress to protect from a like exportation, or other more grievous punishment, the minority of the same body, the legislatures, judges, governors and counsellors of the States, nor their other peaceable inhabitants, who may venture to reclaim the constitutional rights and liberties of the States and people, or who for other causes, good or bad, may be obnoxious to the views, or marked by the suspicions of the President, or be thought dangerous to his or their election, or other interests, public or personal; that the friendless alien has indeed been selected as the safest subject of a first experiment; but the citizen will soon follow, or rather, has already followed, for already has a sedition act marked him as its prey: that these and successive acts of the same character, unless arrested at the threshold, necessarily drive these States into revolution and blood and will furnish new calumnies against republican government, and new pretexts for those who wish it to be believed that man cannot be governed but by a rod of iron: that it would be a dangerous delusion were a confidence in the men of our choice to silence our fears for the safety of our rights: that confidence is everywhere the parent of despotism — free government is founded in jealousy, and not in confidence; it is jealousy and not confidence which prescribes limited constitutions, to bind down those whom we are obliged to trust with power: that our Constitution has accordingly fixed the limits to which, and no further, our confidence may go; and let the honest advocate of confidence read the Alien and Sedition acts, and say if the Constitution has not been wise in fixing limits to the government it created, and whether we should be wise in destroying those limits, Let him say what the government is, if it be not a tyranny, which the men of our choice have conferred on our President, and the President of our choice has assented to, and accepted over the friendly stranger to whom the mild spirit of our country and its law have pledged hospitality and protection: that the men of our choice have more respected the bare suspicion of the President, than the solid right of innocence, the claims of justification, the sacred force of truth, and the forms and substance of law and justice. In questions of powers, then, let no more be heard of confidence in man, but bind him down from mischief by the chains of the Constitution. That this commonwealth does therefore call on its co-States for an expression of their sentiments on the acts concerning aliens and for the punishment of certain crimes herein before specified, plainly declaring whether these acts are or are not authorized by the federal compact. And it doubts not that their sense will be so announced as to prove their attachment unaltered to limited government, whether general or particular. And that the rights and liberties of their co-States will be exposed to no dangers by remaining embarked in a common bottom with their own. That they will concur with this commonwealth in considering the said acts as so palpably against the Constitution as to amount to an undisguised declaration that that compact is not meant to be the measure of the powers of the General Government, but that it will proceed in the exercise over these States, of all powers whatsoever: that they will view this as seizing the rights of the States, and consolidating them in the hands of the General Government, with a power assumed to bind the States (not merely as the cases made federal, casus fœderis but), in all cases whatsoever, by laws made, not with their consent, but by others against* their consent: that this would be to surrender the form of government we have chosen, and live under one deriving its powers from its own will, and not from our authority; and that the co-States, recurring to their natural right in cases not made federal, will concur in declaring these acts void, and of no force, and will each take measures of its own for providing that neither these acts, nor any others of the General Government not plainly and intentionally authorized by the Constitution, shalt be exercised within their respective territories.

9th. Resolved, That the said committee be authorized to communicate by writing or personal conference, at any times or places whatever, with any person or persons who may be appointed by any one or more co-States to correspond or confer with them; and that they lay their proceedings before the next session of Assembly.

The Virginia Resolution of 1798

RESOLVED, That the General Assembly of Virginia, doth unequivocably express a firm resolution to maintain and defend the Constitution of the United States, and the Constitution of this State, against every aggression either foreign or domestic, and that they will support the government of the United States in all measures warranted by the former.

That this assembly most solemnly declares a warm attachment to the Union of the States, to maintain which it pledges all its powers; and that for this end, it is their duty to watch over and oppose every infraction of those principles which constitute the only basis of that Union, because a faithful observance of them, can alone secure it's existence and the public happiness.

That this Assembly doth explicitly and peremptorily declare, that it views the powers of the federal government, as resulting from *the compact, to which the states are parties; as limited by the plain sense and intention of the instrument constituting the compact; as no further valid that they are authorized by the grants enumerated in that compact; and that in case of a deliberate, palpable, and dangerous exercise of other powers, not granted by the said compact, the states who are parties thereto, have the right, and are in duty bound, to interpose for arresting the progress of the evil, and for maintaining within their respective limits, the authorities, rights and liberties appertaining to them.*

That the General Assembly doth also express its deep regret, that a spirit has in sundry instances, been manifested by the federal government, to enlarge its powers by forced constructions of the constitutional charter which defines them; and that implications have appeared of a design to expound certain general phrases (which having been copied from the very limited grant of power, in the former articles of confederation were the less liable to be misconstrued) so as to destroy the meaning and effect, of the particular enumeration which necessarily explains and limits the general phrases; and so as to consolidate the states by degrees, into one sovereignty, the obvious tendency and inevitable consequence of which would be, to transform the present republican system of the United States, into an absolute, or at best a mixed monarchy.

That the General Assembly doth particularly protest against the palpable and alarming infractions of the Constitution, in the two late cases of the "Alien and Sedition Acts" passed at the last session of Congress; the first of which exercises a power no where delegated to the federal government, and which by uniting legislative and judicial powers to those of executive, subverts the general principles of free government; as well as the particular organization, and positive provisions of the federal constitution; and the other of which acts, exercises in like manner, a power not delegated by the constitution, but on the contrary, expressly and positively forbidden by one of the amendments thereto; a power, which more than any other, ought to produce universal alarm, because it is levelled against that right of freely examining public characters and measures, and of free communication among the people thereon, which has ever been justly deemed, the only effectual guardian of every other right.

That this state having by its Convention, which ratified the federal Constitution, expressly declared, that among other essential rights, "the Liberty of Conscience and of the Press cannot be cancelled, abridged, restrained, or modified by any authority of the United States," and from its extreme anxiety to guard these rights from every possible attack of sophistry or ambition, having with other states, recommended an amendment for that purpose, which amendment was, in due time, annexed to the Constitution; it would mark a reproachable inconsistency, and criminal degeneracy, if an indifference were now shewn, to the most palpable violation of one of the Rights, thus declared and secured; and to the establishment of a precedent which may be fatal to the other.

That the good people of this commonwealth, having ever felt, and continuing to feel, the most sincere affection for their brethren of the other states; the truest anxiety for establishing and perpetuating the union of all; and the most scrupulous fidelity to that constitution, which is the pledge of mutual friendship, and the instrument of mutual happiness; the General Assembly doth solemnly appeal to the like dispositions of the other states, in confidence that they will concur with this commonwealth in declaring, as it does hereby declare, that the acts aforesaid, are unconstitutional; and that the necessary and proper measures will be taken by each, for co-operating with this state, in maintaining the Authorities, Rights, and Liberties, referred to the States respectively, or to the people.

That the Governor be desired, to transmit a copy of the foregoing Resolutions to the executive authority of each of the other states, with a request that the same may be communicated to the Legislature thereof; and that a copy be furnished to each of the Senators and Representatives representing this state in the Congress of the United States.

Agreed to by the Senate, December 24, 1798.

The nation as a whole awoke to the danger reflected in the Alien and Sedition Acts. They were allowed to expire in 1800 and 1801, and Thomas Jefferson was elected President and took office in those same years. Jefferson promptly acted to dismantle the many other unconstitutional products of his predecessor's years in power and restore the federal state to its proper role as the minimalist agent of the federated union-state governments. So, we've traveled *that* path before, as well-- and could again.

Anyone up for a stroll?

Obesity Is Not A Public Health Problem
(But Fat-Headedness Is...)
80 CB80 CR

As is so often the case, a few minutes recently spent listening to National Public Radio sufficed to provide me with a subject for a commentary. This liberal organ is a treasure-trove of soft, but often important, targets. In this case, what caught my ear was a story about the increasing incidence of obesity among Americans, which was matter-of-factly presented as a "public health problem".

Obesity is NOT a "public health" problem. It is a personal health problem. Only communicable diseases qualify as having even a *potential* "public" health dimension. If I can't catch it from you, it's not 'our' problem, it's your problem-- and especially if it's behavior-related or behavior-remediable. By no means can a non-communicable, personally-controllable condition such as obesity qualify as being public-health related.

However, what is really meant by the NPR characterization is that obesity is a health-related *financial* problem, with a public-policy dimension. This is based upon the proposition that eventually society will be obliged to spend extra money remediating the ill effects of self-destructive overeating and sloth, which therefore brings either the behavior, or external factors which contribute to it, properly into the ambit of public decision-making. This is a standard example of tail-wagging-the-dog reasoning.

In this case, society's completely optional inclination toward charity (the tail) is used as a pretext to legitimize its assertion of authority over anything which might stimulate that inclination (the dog). It never occurs to those who make this argument that society can simply forego its inclination toward charity, and that to do so is infinitely more ethical than claiming tyrannical authority over individuals in order to prevent occasions for indulging that inclination from arising in the first place.

Still, even if the logical fallacy and moral bankruptcy of this formula go unchallenged, the simplest of clear-eyed analyses establishes that, from no more than an utterly pragmatic perspective, the opposite of what the dog-waggers suggest is actually the case. Obesity is anything BUT a public financial problem-- and particularly within this wagged-dog context.

After all, that context necessarily embraces regular old-age-related welfare outlays such as 'Social Security' and 'Medicare' to an endless stream of beneficiaries. Because one of the effects of obesity is an early death, the lifetime consumption of Social Security benefits by the obese as a class is considerably lower than it otherwise would be. Thus, as long as Social Security is in the picture, obesity is actually a net benefit to the public finance.

The same is true regarding Medicare. The obese-- like the fit-- conduct the vast majority of their overall health-care resource consumption as their lives are winding to a close. There are two reasons why this is true: age-related incapacity, and lingering illness. Since the obese rarely, if ever, make it to an extremity of age at which incapacity becomes a problem, and tend to succumb to illness quickly rather than hold it at bay (once at an age to qualify for Medicare), end-of-life related outlays for the obese also tend to be much less than those made on behalf of the healthy.

So, all in all, obesity is anything BUT a 'public problem', whether viewed from a health *or* a financial perspective. However, there *is* a public-health dimension to its mischaracterization.

After all, few things are more supportive of general health than is general wealth, and little is more systemically destructive of general wealth than subjecting individual choice-making to political interference-- which is to say, subordinating the choices of some Americans to the interests of whichever of their neighbors have gained control of the political apparatus, whether under the pretext of controlling public 'charitable' outlays, or for any other reason. The relentless decline of every polity which has succumbed to such foolishness testifies to this simple and straightforward reality: Societal prosperity (and thus, overall well-being) is maximized-- spontaneously, and exclusively-- when each person is left alone to make his own decisions and look out for his own interests.

Only under conditions of maximum freedom can the millions of information signals, and reward feedbacks, which are the key to high levels of universal personal productivity be accurately (and thus usefully) generated and injected into the economic matrix. Political interference overrides those signals, requiring participants in the economy to make choices which are not actually responsive to its data. Those artificially skewed choices inject distortion, and a consequent reduction in efficiency, into the overall system. Thus, to allow yet another incremental expansion of governmental control is to diminish the polity's wealth, and in turn, its health-- by reducing its aggregate ability to research and develop weight-control products, for instance; or its individual member's ability to finance the leisure time needed for fitness training.

Rich polities like America are prone to the kind of sloppiness and distraction that invite political interference in the economy-- but such interferences cannot be afforded for long. Sooner or later, the distortions introduced into the economic matrix come to dominate, and what had been a harmonious free-form concert becomes a much poorer cacophony. Such an afflicted economy won't necessarily collapse, but every participant-- other than those manipulating the political process to skew the choices of others-- will get less for their efforts than they otherwise would and should.

Of course, the manipulators actually do BETTER in the cacophony than they otherwise would (at least in the short run), and thus it is in their interest to keep the rest of us acclimated to the inefficiencies of discord. As a result, we are treated to the sort of idiotic pontifications of NPR that inspired this commentary. Also as a result, we are seeing an increasingly rapid and sophisticated formulation of the public-relations campaign and the novel, custom-fitted legal theory intended to truss up another victim for the furnishing of a blood-meal to the same parasitic class of lawyers and politicians that developed its tastes on the tobacco and medical-silicone industries.

It would be an intolerable groaner to exploit the opportunity presented here for references to these slimy special interests as seeking to "live off the fat of the land,"-- and so I will regretfully content myself with this one contrivance alone. I *am* sufficiently shameless to observe that the dynamic outlined above-- an early practice of sharp-eyed and disciplined clear thinking resulting in a prosperity which, a generation or so later, is thoughtlessly wallowed in, while crippling corruption takes hold unnoticed-- can be usefully expressed as a run of self-indulgent 'fat' years followed as surely as night follows day by a run of 'lean'.

America is a long way down this ruinous path already. We're not quite past the point of no return, but turning around and climbing back the slope down which we have come will be hard work. But, hey-- as we are so unctuously reminded by NPR and its fellow-travelers, we can use the exercise.

Barbarians Inside The Gates
ഗ©ൽ©ൽ

If they really meant it, those questioning the humanity of human embryos in the debate regarding federal funding of embryonic stem cell research would reveal how utterly worthless a typical or even a 'privileged' academic education has become in our time. Because they don't, what is instead revealed is how good has been the indoctrination in moral relativism, self-absorption, and nihilism in government-run and government-influenced schools, as the "Me Generations"-- having become conscious of the approaching infirmities of age-- look to the dismemberment of their very young as a source of possible escape.

Rather than addressing the relevant issues with sincerity, the pro-human-guinea-pig side is engaging in a grotesquely cynical exercise intended to conceal the simple fact that they *don't care* that human embryos are obviously human. They care only that something they value can be gotten at the expense of others-- others who can't defend themselves or even protest. (Also, of course, many of them care very much that to concede intellectual ground here would be dangerous to the abortion industry and the painstakingly- constructed delusional view of reality upon which it depends.)

Arguments of varying degrees of cunning and depravity have been deployed in an effort to tart up the naked selfishness at work here. Among these are that because a very early stage person requires a nurturing and protective environment for survival, its humanity is only potential, not actual. It should not be necessary to point out that by way of this argument the "humanity" of most people up to adolescence; in extreme old age or severe disability; or otherwise in a condition of helplessness could be viewed as properly subject to another's self-interested judgment. Plainly stated, the evil of this argument is clear, however inconvenient its acknowledgement may be.

The reductio ad absurdum converse variation of this argument has also been trotted out: That if a very early stage person must be accorded its heritage as a human being, then so too must every human cell, since (as this sophistry would have it) it has the potential to become a complete person through cloning. This is just low-brow nonsense, deployed to clutter up the mental landscape with both an errant biological proposition, and the logical error of "false choice". Of course a cell which is a component of an individual person is NOT capable of becoming another person, any more than is an ovum or sperm until a fundamental change has taken place through both of them merging into a self-directed, developing entity.

Such a cell, regardless of the environment or the nurturing afforded it, is not a human being and will never become one. If a human hair cell or skin cell or the like *is* used in a cloning procedure, with the result being a self-directed developing individual (leaving the question of the propriety of such a procedure for another day), that individual will also then be fully entitled to status as a human. But the cell itself never will be.

Further, even if such cells WERE capable of independent development into discrete individual humans, this fact would in no way impose functional paralysis upon society, as those who present this contention slyly intend for us to unconsciously suspect. The essence of this aspect of the ploy is that if we have come to moral terms with clipping our hair and fingernails, then we have crossed the ethical Rubicon and have no standing from which to balk at similarly depraved treatment of embryos, which are merely a higher order of the same class of creature. The reciprocal side of this false choice, also calculated to erode our moral purpose, is that if we insist on enshrining as inviolate the rights of embryonic humans, then we must do so in the case of the referenced organic detritus as well, and who would want to live in THAT inconvenient world?!

Another position taken in support of the practice is rooted in the fact that many embryos are currently produced through the *in vitro* fertilization process and subsequently destroyed or abandoned. To use these embryos in research, goes the argument, in no way worsens their fate, and derives a possible positive outcome from their demise, albeit one from which they will not personally benefit.

This is a most strange argument, unless one is immersed in the same degenerate utilitarian context as those offering it. Clearly the overarching response to the facts presented therein is to immediately and with horror abandon the production of these "surplus" children, and the *in vitro* procedure itself, if necessary!

Other arguments abound, all equally mired in self-interest without scruples. An alternate glimpse of the character behind them all can be had when the pro-side must address the counter-argument favoring the use of consensually obtained adult stem cells. All that is offered is that adult stem cells are more expensive to process and appear, at this early stage in the research, less generous in the range of their possible benefits.

That's the sum of it. They cost more and might not work as well, to boot-- so keep bringing those babies.

*****

It may be that there is a legitimate argument that could be made which would justify the use of these human babies for a higher good. To judge by the amount of fraud, camouflage, and illogic that that position's supporters appear to feel they must use to make their case, I'm not holding my breath until it's been demonstrated.

Instead, I'm holding my nose. In the Dark Ages, it was popularly believed that witches and warlocks ate babies in order to extend their lifespan or regain their youth. The practice was, of course, condemned as a heinous evil. I would have hoped that, here in the 21st century, there would have been no question as to our maintaining at least this same rudimentary level of morality and respect for human dignity.

Sadly, this is not so. Our technology has become god-like, but our morality has degenerated into squalid, self-indulgent barbarism.

About Weapons of Mass Destruction
ᗏᘓᑕᘔᗑᘓᑕᘔ

Citing-- with no apparent sense of irony-- the dangers of the possible deployment within our borders of weapons of mass destruction, the U.S. government is seeking to acquire vastly broadened authority over the people. Powers sought include substantially enhanced license to wiretap; to open bank accounts and tax records to law enforcement scrutiny; to use secret evidence against suspects, and much more.

As we consider our reaction to this effort, it is wise to reflect on the fact that the most devastating weapon-of-mass-destruction ever deployed against any particular national population has always been its own unrestrained government, armed with powers ceded during moments of real or imagined crisis. The consolidations of several such panic-driven concessions into rigid oligarchies or dictatorships during just the last century alone slaughtered more than 170,000,000. These recent examples of the consequences of trading liberty for security-- and the certain fact that our American experience is a fragile oasis of freedom and general prosperity in the vast desert of serfdom and poverty which is the historic norm for 99% of humankind in all times and places-- should serve as a caution against both haste, and a reliance on the good intentions (or discretion and longevity) of those who seek new or renewed delegations of power.

Furthermore, any assertion that the new authorities being requested will forestall future attacks is specious and demagogic. It is obvious that any future assault will accommodate itself in design and target to whatever measures of security are currently in place, just as did the last; and the demeanor of the perpetrators will be shaped to suit the existing protocols as well.

While it is possible to cite numerous problems with the adherence to legal particulars on the part of the suicide bombers responsible for last month's atrocities, such as being in the country on expired visas and the like, all of them were clearly within the tolerance range of the then current level of enforcement. If we begin to scrupulously enforce such requirements, we can rest assured that future suicide bombers will scrupulously adhere to them, and then proceed within that context. Those requirements would not have spared the past victims and will not protect future victims, and even if the tightening of security at airports makes targeting aircraft less viable, plenty of other targets abound.

It should, in fact, be obvious (and should be presumed to be obvious) to those whom we pay to be experts on such matters that granting the sought-after new powers to the government will not suffice to make us proof against attack-- or even marginally safer. Nonetheless, our "experts" tirelessly urge us on. The best that can be said for such efforts is that they allow these highly paid "experts" to seem proactive, and thus prop up their incumbencies; but the satisfaction of that narrow interest is-- needless to say-- a poor justification for delivering more power into the hands of the state. Under the circumstances, suspicion as to the sincerity or true character of their motives is not at all out of line.

For instance, Senator Charles Schumer recently advocated imposing the security rituals now common to airline travel upon rail passengers. I may be wrong, but it seems to me that if a train becomes the object of terrorist interest, such an interest could be satisfied most effectively without ever boarding the train-- unless it has escaped my notice that trains no longer use tracks.

So, maybe Schumer's just an idiot. Or, maybe he just knows someone who'll pay a lot of money for the Amtrak customer list that his proposal would create if enacted, and he's figured a way to get a cut. Perhaps he's just engaging in some political opportunism by which he gets some free media at the risk of the rest of us being pointlessly inconvenienced, invaded, and burdened with a new and permanent expense in exchange for no benefit at all-- which is to say, he gets a benefit and we get the bill.

*****

Of course, there are measures that can be taken which DO hold the promise of substantially reducing American vulnerability to the dangers posed by terrorism. In a wonderful synchronicity, such measures are uniquely available to Americans as a consequence of that same monumental productivity responsible for the poisonous envy and hatred animating our enemies. Taking advantage of the opportunity which they represent would reduce the concentration of power currently enjoyed by the political elite, however, so it is safe to say that these measures will enjoy no advocacy from that quarter.

Thus, even while crews still labor to comb and clear the rubble of the Pentagon and the World Trade Center, and mourning continues among the families of the victims, the posture of that elite is to encourage brave talk of rebuilding and carrying on as before, rather than to think creatively. Get back to business as usual, they urge, and raise up another grand symbol of American greatness, confident that it can successfully be spared from becoming another mass grave by the steps toward a police state which they DO advocate. America is strong and great, they tell us, and will not bow to aggression. Fair enough; true enough; and proper enough.

But the real strength and greatness of America lies not in our ability to clamp down on the freedoms which set us apart from the rest of the world, but rather in our flexibility and our imagination; and our ability and willingness to adapt to and maximize the benefit of new challenges and new opportunities. Right now, our challenge and opportunity lies in thinking, and living, outside of the box.

Consider this: 32,000,000 U.S. workers do not report to a dense-packed ground zero five mornings a week; and the parents of as many as 5,000,000 (maybe considerably more) school-age children decline to have their kids spend each day in a high-casualty-potential target. This is because the American entrepreneurial dynamo has generated a high-tech infrastructure in which telecommuting and homeschooling are perfectly viable and widely exercised options, the benefits of which could be, and would be, being enjoyed by vastly larger numbers-- if everyone were aware of the possibilities.

Rather than urging Americans to support new police powers which certainly diminish liberty in exchange for an uncertain promise to make safe our continuing to crowd into big buildings each day, the administration and Congress should be using the bully pulpit to sing the praises of working at home, of teleconferencing, and of homeschooling. Not only would we become immensely harder targets for attacks by our enemies, we also would reap enormous additional benefits: in quality of life in general; in the education of our children; in our environmental impact; and in our cost of living.

Here's an immediate example of what IS being done, and what could and should be done: Right now, the discovery that anthrax-laden envelopes have been delivered to multiple targets around the country has public officials issuing instructions on how best to identify and deal with high-risk hard-copy mail. Why not simply stop using hard-copy mail for the business and junk correspondence which is the variety susceptible to tampering? (Personal letters are generally not a risk as the handwriting and return addresses are familiar guarantors of its provenance and trustworthiness to the recipient). Email is absolutely proof against infecting anyone with anything, and the danger to computers associated with it are due in large part to poor practices by both senders and receivers, which would be easily minimized by a few public service announcements and standardized practices on the part of service providers.

Another substantial benefit of this cultural judo would be the improvement in our civic lives. Not only would citizens have more time with their families, but they would have more time available in which to stay abreast of public policy issues and to thoughtfully express themselves both amongst their fellows and at the ballot box. American greatness was conceived and nurtured by a rural, decentralized society, and while we will never again quite duplicate that earlier structure, the massive densely-packed population centers, with their chronic social pathologies and corrupt machine politics, can and should be greatly diminished.

In addition to encouraging Americans to embrace the opportunities and benefits of decentralizing their work and school lives, our leaders should be directing public attention and support to the refinement and deployment of private energy production. The technology by which every home could provide for its own electricity, through solar concentrating generators and fuel cell systems, not to mention straight natural gas fired generators and other systems, has long been available. Vigorously encouraging the adoption of this technology, would minimize or eliminate the potential for massive disruptions through terrorist targeting of centralized power systems.

Similarly, Congress should reject out of hand the scheme of various state governments to form a compact, or cartel, in order to impose sales taxes on internet commerce, a formula for discouraging this immensely safer method of shopping. Instead, congress should make permanent its ban on internet taxation on the national level, and resolve to withhold its necessary cooperation (such compacts are unconstitutional without congressional approval) from the conspiring state governments.

Of course, many special interests can be counted on to howl with protest at the implementation of each of these notions, such as the public education industry, the road repair industry, the political bosses, the postal unions, and assorted busybodies who will find it much more difficult to intimidate and harass companies and workers when workforces are spread over hundreds of square miles and children are safe under the watchful eyes of their parents. And certainly, not every workplace can be dispersed. But a huge percentage can, and of the type that cannot, such as manufacturing facilities, micro-plants are already out-competing the behemoths of the past, and can continue to make up a larger and larger share of their respective industries, thus minimizing unavoidable concentrations of personnel and key industrial capacity.

*****

While much may have changed on September 11th, one thing that did not is the proper relationship between Americans and their government, and that is not the area in which adjustments to any new reality should be made. Those currently under consideration will not accomplish their stated goals, and might do much mischief. As William Pitt said, *"Necessity is the plea for every infringement of human freedom. It is the argument of tyrants; it is the creed of slaves"*.

That we must adjust is undeniable; that we should do so thoughtfully, creatively, and with enduring faith in the transcendent ability of our system of free enterprise and individual sovereignty to overcome adversity is just as certain. Our system is not strong for being able to absorb encroachments on liberty without harm-- it cannot, for such encroachments in and of themselves eat away at its sinews. Rather it is strong because by the very disdain for encroachment which is its foundation it taps and focuses the inexhaustible resources of the human mind and spirit against which no dark and cramped envy or hatred can prevail.

So let's flex these big muscles of ours, to enhance our security and dismay our enemies. But in so doing, let's especially flex the ones in our heads.

*****

Afterword

"The whole aim of practical politics is to keep the populace alarmed—and hence clamorous to be led to safety—by menacing it with an endless series of hobgoblins, all of them imaginary."
-H.L. Mencken

In the four years since the preceding words were written, one thing has become clear: No war is, or ever was, being made upon America by terrorists. The making of war is the making of a sustained series of destructive efforts against a target. Although America has suffered a sustained assault of hyperbolic, mindless fear-mongering on the subject by the federal government (with the enthusiastic support of much of the profit-driven media, and the occasional contributory gesture from a state or local government in line for a helping of

"Homeland Security" federal grant money), there has been no follow-up to the Sept. 11th, 2001 event, despite endless opportunities against which no preventative measures are possible. Thus, while it may not be possible to say exactly what the heinous crimes committed on September 11th, 2001 really were, it IS possible to say that they were NOT acts of war.

Since no war OF terrorism (or by terrorists) is being made upon America, as little as this alone and simple logic suffice to demonstrate that America is not engaged in a war AGAINST terrorism (or terrorists). (Both are ridiculous constructions in any case: "Terrorism" is a means, and a "terrorist" is merely a member of a general class; neither term properly describes or identifies an enemy. Such constructions are used *because* they are vague, of course; they provide for adopting a military demeanor against any future target of choice, since none has been previously identified.)

What America IS engaged in is a significant flare-up of the now century-and-a-half old war of the ambitious beneficiaries of an unrestricted central government against the restraints of the Constitution and the Rule of Law. We allow ourselves to be blinded to, or distracted from, this reality at our extreme peril. Only a child or a fool would have failed to observe that power once ceded to government is never again relinquished without the shedding of blood, sweat and tears-- and especially when the power given is of a character such as to facilitate the repression of dissent, such as that upon which the enemies of liberty are currently focusing by means of instruments like the 'Patriot Act' and 'The Real ID Act'. The powers sought by these measures are those necessary to the erection and sustenance of a police-state, and nothing less.

Cry out in opposition now, or cry out in misery and despair later. Does that sound hyperbolic? Study history.

More importantly, stand up and act. I invite and implore everyone reading these words to join the growing ranks of those Americans who are courageously and successfully insisting that the United States and the several state governments abide by the letter of the law (and who are thereby regaining enormous power over their own property and the uses to which it is put). To learn more about this critically important effort to restore the balance of power intended by America's founders, visit losthorizons.com.

Even Solitary Candles, Once Lit, Can Roll Back The Darkness

(Adapted from a speech given to the Colorado State Libertarian Convention, May 23rd 2004)

ℰ℧ℭℨℰ℧ℭℛ

"I am only one, but I am one. I cannot do everything, but I can do something. And because I cannot do everything, I will not refuse to do the something that I can do. What I can do, I should do. And what I should do, by the grace of God, I will do."

-- Edward Everett Hale

Good afternoon. First of all, I'd like to thank Bo Schaeffer, Elizabeth Johnson, and all of you, for inviting me to join you at this gathering of patriots. I am honored. You are among those to whom the torch first kindled by the likes of Samuel Adams, Thomas Jefferson, and Tom Paine has passed. Being with you today is good.

I'm here specifically to talk with you about the income tax, and I'm going to get squarely into that subject in a moment. I'd like to start, however, with a few words regarding a somewhat different area of law, which I think will both be of general interest, and will also prove useful in setting the stage for what will follow.

The 9th circuit court of appeals, which many observers feel has racked up a lot to answer for over the years in terms of bad-- if not wacky-- decisions, bought itself a whole lot of redemption recently. Ruling late last year and again in March in a case known as Raich versus Ashcroft, the court enjoined the federal Drug Enforcement Agency from engaging in activities aimed at suppressing California's medical marihuana initiative. In so doing, the 9th circuit court has significantly served the cause of the rule of law in America.

The authority under which the DEA operates is the Interstate Commerce Clause of Article 1, section 8 of the United States Constitution, which provides Congress with the power to regulate commerce among the states. "The Congress shall have power... to regulate commerce with foreign nations, and among the several states, and with the Indian tribes." This is obviously a very limited power. First of all, and undeniably, this power is confined in its reach to 'commerce', and only such commerce as involves two or more of the several states. Thomas Jefferson, discussing a proposal to create a national bank, expressed the nature of the authority granted by the commerce clause this way:

> "...if this was [alleged to be] *an exercise of the power of regulating commerce, it would be void, as extending as much to the internal commerce of every State, as to its external. For the power given to Congress by the Constitution does not extend to the internal regulation of the commerce of a State, (that is to say of the commerce between citizen and citizen,) which remain exclusively with its own legislature; but to its external commerce only, that is to say, its commerce with another State, or with foreign nations, or with the Indian tribes."*

John Marshall, first chief justice of the United States Supreme Court described his understanding of the meaning and limitations of the commerce clause in the 1824 case of Gibbons versus Ogden with these words:

> *"It is not intended to say that these words comprehend that* [type of] *commerce, which is completely internal, which is carried on between man and man in a State, or between different parts of the same State, and which does not extend to or affect other States. Such a power would be inconvenient, and is certainly unnecessary."*
> *"Comprehensive as the word `among' is, it may very properly be restricted to that commerce which concerns more States than one. . . . The enumeration presupposes something not enumerated; and that something, if we regard the language or the subject of the sentence, must be the exclusively internal commerce of a State."*

The limitation of the application of that power to agencies of the several state governments exclusively is more ambiguous, perhaps-- but according to James Madison, the chief architect of the Constitution, the purpose of the clause is *"the relief of the States which import and export through other States, from the improper contributions levied on them by the latter"*-- in other words, preventing one State from taxing goods passing through it into another. Taking Madison at his word, and bearing in mind that the Constitution is, technically, a compact between, and in regard to, the several states acting in their corporate capacities-- it could be argued that the commerce clause has no direct application to the actions of private citizens at all, even actions involving `commerce' between two such citizens across state borders. Seen in this light, such actions would be subject only to the authority of the respective state governments, with that authority in turn subordinate to that of the federal government to ensure that such commerce is unimpeded. In practical fact, this understanding of the clause reigned more-or-less unchallenged for the first 100 years or more of American history.

During the era of progressivist influence in America-- essentially the first half of the 20th century, a naïve popular faith in the capacity of democratic politics was exploited by rapacious special interests which recognized the opportunities afforded by a government of unlimited power to those who could influence or control its actions. These interests seized upon several elements in the language or construction of the federal Constitution which can be seen as ambiguous, if taken out of context, as the instruments of their ambitions. Prominent among these was the commerce clause. The original theory under which latitude was found in the clause was that if Congress is authorized to regulate interstate commerce, it can reasonably assert authority over things which *affect* interstate commerce.

This notion found its most promiscuous expression in a Supreme Court ruling in 1942 in the case of Wickard versus Filburn, in which the court accepted the federal government's argument that because the wheat a farmer grew *for his own consumption* reduced the amount that he himself would otherwise be obliged to buy, such production affected local commerce, which in turn affected regional, and ultimately interstate commerce in that commodity-- thus making his decision to plant his own wheat something over which the feds had lawful authority. Sound absurd and indefensible? It is the regime under which all but the very oldest here have lived for our entire lives.

Happily, this regime is now crumbling. The correction began in 1995 with the decision in United States versus Lopez, in which the Supreme Court overturned a federal gun control measure criminalizing possession of a gun within 1000 feet of a school. As is true of most federal criminal statutes, this one was being enforced within the several states under the auspices of the commerce clause, a stretch which Lopez bravely and wisely challenged.

The defense offered by the government actually tried to break somewhat new ground from that previously tilled under the clause, since not even as indirect a commerce connection as that deployed to stop farmer Filburn from growing his own wheat could plausibly be proposed for the simple possession of a gun. So, the federal attorneys suggested instead that since the parts from which such guns are made had (presumably) at one time traveled in interstate commerce, and involved manufacturing capacity, which, on an aggregate basis had a national scope, governmental authority over the gun-- and therefore its owner-- existed, essentially forever and in all circumstances. The court rejected this contention wholesale. In its ruling, the court cites John Marshall's language in Gibbons versus Ogden, regarding the limitation of the clause to matters purely interstate, and then goes on to observe:

> *Similarly, under the Government's "national productivity" reasoning, Congress could regulate any activity that it found was related to the economic productivity of individual citizens: family law (including marriage, divorce, and child custody), for example. Under the theories that the Government presents in support of 922(q)* [the law in question]*, it is difficult to perceive any limitation on federal power, even in areas such as criminal law enforcement or education where States historically have been sovereign. Thus, if we were to accept the Government's arguments, we are hard-pressed to posit any activity by an individual that Congress is without power to regulate."*

Shortly after this decision, the court repeats essentially the same perspective in striking down a federal assault law, holding that, although the actors whose behavior the government was attempting to reach might be personally involved in interstate commerce, and may even be arguably inhibited in such involvement by the acts being proscribed, it is an unsupportable stretch of the commerce clause power to thus extend it over individual behavior. In this ruling the court makes another strong statement reflecting its growing intolerance for legislative adventurism in defiance of the clear meaning of Constitutional language:

> *"Congress found that gender-motivated violence affects interstate commerce "by deterring potential victims from traveling interstate, from engaging in employment in interstate business, and from transacting with business, and in places involved in interstate commerce;..." " Given these findings and petitioner's arguments, the concern that we expressed in Lopez that Congress might use the Commerce Clause to completely obliterate the Constitution's distinction between national and local authority seems well founded"*

That same year, the court also threw out a long-standing federal law against arson, again rejecting expansive federal claims of authority under the commerce clause.

Now, following in the wake of this refreshing Supreme Court trend, comes the 9th circuit court serving up what may well prove to be the coup-de-grace for the commerce clause's contributions to the exercise of unlimited power by the federal government. Certainly, its recent pair of rulings in Raich versus Ashcroft represent a powerful blow to that regime.

The basic facts of the case are fairly simple. The plaintiffs, Angel McClary Raich and several associates, grow, supply, and consume marijuana in California, enjoying protection from state harassment by the provisions of the California Medical Marijuana Initiative.

That initiative has not dissuaded the federal DEA from abusing them, however, under the auspices of the Controlled

Substances Act-- itself an appendage of the Federal Food and Drug Act, which is one of the oldest federal enactments created under the mantle of the commerce clause. The enactment of the Federal Food and Drug Act, in fact, predates many of the wild flights of fancy tolerated by the Supreme Court in Wickard and similar cases, and the legislation contains its own statutory definition of 'interstate commerce'; one far more consistent with the founder's views than current administration practices conducted under its authority would suggest. That definition, by the terms of which all federal drug law enforcement is circumscribed, declare 'interstate commerce' to be:

> *(1) commerce between any State or Territory and any place outside thereof, and*
> *(2) commerce within the District of Columbia or within any other Territory not organized with a legislative body,...*

It is self-evident by the terms of this definition-- even without looking to the higher law of the Constitution-- that the private, in-state growth and consumption of marijuana, or anything else, is outside the purview of this and any dependent federal law such as the Controlled Substances Act. But the DEA is accustomed to friendly, if not compliant courts; more significantly it is accustomed to ignorant adversaries unaware of the details and limitations of the law. Therefore it proceeded with its high-handed business-as-usual against these peaceable Californians. Raich and her friends, knowing at least the Constitution, if not the nuances of the Federal Food and Drug Act, sought an injunction in the federal courts against future assaults by the agency.

The government, faced with another case involving a completely locally grown, distributed, and consumed item, offered-- concept for concept, if not word for word-- the very argument it used 62 years ago in Wickard versus Filburn. Indeed, in crafting the Controlled Substances Act, or CSA,

Congress included a lengthy preamble describing its 'findings' that the substances-- and the Americans who use them-- over which it wished to exercise power by way of the act partake of the same ephemeral interstate commerce connections and influences which won the day in the Wickard case so long ago. However, recognizing that such 'findings' carry little legal weight and that the CSA remains circumscribed by the Constitution's language, as well as that within the Food and Drug Act itself, the 9th circuit court, said no, twice.

The appellate court's ruling was not so bold as to cleanly embrace the clarity of Marshall, Madison, or Jefferson, in that it largely confines its focus to the definition of 'commerce', observing that none is involved in the private production and consumption of Raich's marijuana, while dancing around the 'among the states' element of the statute. Even so, the ruling upholds the principle that the words of the law must be given no more and no less than their meaning, and represents a significant step down the path charted by the Supreme Court in Lopez.

Raich versus Ashcroft will now go to the Supreme Court, which only last year extended an invitation to the circuit courts for just such a case. Not only is there every reason to expect the high court to be predisposed to uphold the lower court's ruling, but even if the supremes were inclined to reverse their own recent doctrine, they would have great difficulty overcoming the correctness of the circuit court's reasoning. Thus, a highly significant reining-in of long-standing congressional excess is probably imminent. This will not instantly undo all legislation promulgated under the elastic reading of the commerce clause, but will likely deal much of it an at least slowly fatal wound.

*****

I have begun with this discussion of the commerce clause and the jurisprudence associated with it in order to illustrate several important realities. First and foremost is that a great deal of what is typically understood to be true about the law, particularly federal law-- and about federal jurisdiction-- is wrong.

Although you are a group far more conscious of matters of law than most Americans, I venture to say that many in this room did not know, or at least were not confident in their suspicion, that the federal government has almost no direct criminal jurisdiction of any kind in the several union states. It is only by connivance and craft, making claims-- credible or incredible-- on the basis of some narrow Constitutionally-granted authority such as those we have just examined that the feds attempt to exercise jurisdiction.

We've talked about federal arson, assault, and 'possession of a gun in a school-zone' legislation as predicating its authority on a ridiculous stretch of the commerce clause-- did you know that even the federal criminalizing of possession of a firearm by a felon, one of the most grey-bearded and seemingly solid expressions of federal police power, only applies within the several states as a commerce clause measure? Even before Lopez, charges of felon-in-possession directed against knowledgeable and courageous citizens were being thrown out by federal judges as outside of federal authority. As in all such cases, of course, reliance upon the limits of the Constitution, or those crafted into lesser statutes, such as the definition of 'interstate commerce' in the Food and Drug Act, are available only to those who know the law and are bold enough to demand its protection.

Another lesson to be learned from looking at the commerce clause history is that either the law means what it says, or there is no law. As the Supreme Court expressed in the relevant rulings cited, the door opened by promiscuous latitude in the interpretation of the words of a statute leads to an alien universe of unlimited governmental power. In so doing, they say nothing new, but merely echo wisdom of such ancient standing that even Confucious, two thousand five hundred years ago, observed that *"When words lose their meaning, people lose their liberty."*

The essence of law is clarity, predictability, and limitation. We do not create law in order to wonder about its meaning, or to give power over that meaning to interpreters; and we do not craft law to grant latitude, but rather, to limit it. This principle, that the words of a statute must be given their plain meaning, is one of the most firmly established in American law. Here is another United States Supreme Court cite, from Connally versus General Construction Company:

> *"...a statute which either forbids or requires the doing of an act in terms so vague that men of common intelligence must necessarily guess at its meaning and differ as to its application violates the first essential of due process of law."*

A third important reality demonstrated by the history of the commerce clause is that Americans get the restraint in government that they pay for. It is daunting and costly to contest the expansive interpretations of government power favored by its advocates, but unless it is contested, that expansiveness will prevail. As Jefferson observed, *"It is the natural course of things for government to gain ground, and liberty to yield."*

On the other hand, if it IS contested that expansiveness can be curtailed. It may be hard to believe, but as I suggested a moment ago, many litigants, even those assisted by highly paid and well-respected counsel, proceed through legal contests-- even landmark legal contests the course of which takes the battle into the Supreme Court-- without ever invoking, or often even knowing, the actual words of the statutes whose application they are contesting.

Instead, it is common for a case to be argued solely against or about the merits of whatever may be the current relevant paradigm-- its apparent fairness, or utility, or even its utility in service to a different paradigm, in a tail-wagging-the-dog formula such as those that defend motorcycle helmet requirements on the theory that helmet use reduces the burden upon government-provided health-care. This is because many people suffer from an unfortunate reluctance to think outside the box, even when the box is just the efforts of a competing interest to control the terms of the debate; and because most professionals, in law as in all other specialties, have found that rocking the boat is a bad career move-- or at least makes for a harder day's work than just playing along with the status quo. Yet when a challenge IS offered, when someone like Lopez, or Jones, or Raich refuses to play along-- that is to say, when such litigants pay the price for more restraint in government-- it can be achieved.

The final, and most practically significant reality illustrated in this discussion of the commerce clause litigations that I wish to point out before turning directly to the income tax is that, despite the efforts of paradigm-shifters to muddy or mutate the meaning of various laws, the actual federal legislative product still typically conforms to the limits imposed by the Constitution. However much Congress may want to conduct a war on drugs, for instance, it has never revisited section 321 of the Federal Food and Drug Act and changed the definition of 'interstate commerce' by which all drug-related legislation is limited; nor has it ever created a custom definition solely for the purposes of the Controlled Substances Act.

An equivalent legislative restraint will be found in all federal enactments of any significant tenure-- those restraints are simply buried deep among thousands or hundreds of thousands of words in a statutory structure the exploration of which was, typically, abandoned by the legal profession long ago. After all, not only does Congress hate the idea of its limited authority being made manifest by the Supreme Court ruling which would inevitably follow such an overstep, but generally, it has been sufficient for Congressional purposes that most Americans are too uninstructed or intimidated to invoke the Constitutional or subordinate statutory limitations on federal legislation.

*****

Federal legislation based upon the Commerce Clause draws on a Constitutional grant of authority-- but one which is, as the courts are lately reminding us, limited in its scope. The federal taxing power is also a limited authority, and is, in fact, the *most* limited authority. Unlike the Commerce Clause-- in which the limits are found through implication, and by analysis of the meaning of the words used in constructing the clause-- the limits on the taxing power are not only explicit and independent of the authorizing clause, but, insofar as the prohibition against unapportioned direct taxes is concerned, it is the only explicit limit imposed on a grant of Congressional authority which is expressed twice in the Constitution-- first at Article 1 Section 2:

> "*...direct Taxes shall be apportioned among the several States which may be included within*

this Union, according to their respective
numbers,..."

and, even more forcefully in Section 9:

"No capitation, or other direct, Tax shall be laid,
unless in Proportion to the Census or
Enumeration herein before directed to be
taken."

We often joke about the apparent need to
perfect the Supreme Court's understanding of
Constitutional intent by the addition of the phrase, "And
we really mean it!" here and there throughout the
document. This is an older idea than many of us
realize, as is made clear by the repetition of the
prohibition against unapportioned direct taxes. This is
the one the Founders really meant.

Immediately, of course, the question of the
meaning of 'direct tax' arises. Black's law dictionary
offers this definition:

"One which is demanded from the very persons
who it is intended or desired should pay it."

A more illuminating definition can be had from
looking at the meaning of the one type of direct tax to
which the Founders specifically referred, a capitation.
Bouvier's 1856 Dictionary of Constitutional Law defines
a capitation as:

"...an imposition which is yearly laid on each
person according to his estate and ability."

Adam Smith, the father of economics and the
reigning authority on this and all related subjects at the
time of the framing of the Constitution describes
capitations with greater clarity, saying, in part:

"The taxes which, it is intended, should fall indifferently upon every different species of revenue, are capitation taxes,"... *"Capitation taxes, if it is attempted to proportion them to the fortune or revenue of each contributor, become altogether arbitrary. The state of a man's fortune varies from day to day, and without an inquisition more intolerable than any tax, and renewed at least once every year, can only be guessed at."...* *"Capitation taxes, so far as they are levied upon the lower ranks of people, are direct taxes upon the wages of labour, and are attended with all the inconveniences of such taxes."...* *"In the capitation which has been levied in France without any interruption since the beginning of the present century, the highest orders of people are rated according to their rank by an invariable tariff; the lower orders of people, according to what is supposed to be their fortune, by an assessment which varies from year to year."*

Clearly any tax which falls upon *"every different species of revenue"*, *"the wages of labour"*, or, *"what is supposed to be [anyone's] fortune"* as measured by *"an assessment which varies from year to year."* is a capitation. Clearly such taxes cannot be imposed except by apportionment.

And you know what? They're not. In fact, such taxes are not imposed in America today at all.

Such taxes are remitted, such taxes are collected, such taxes are browbeaten and intimidated and connived out of millions of Americans every year, but they are not imposed by any law. And this disconnect between the actual existing legal structure and what is practically administered upon the American people is not one dependent upon elastic and fanciful arguments about interrelationships and influences as has been the case in the interpretations of commerce clause legislation.

Federal revenue law is quite explicit as to what it seeks to tax, and *"every different species of revenue"*, *"the wages of labour"*, or, *"what is supposed to be [anyone's] fortune"* as measured by *"an assessment which varies from year to year."* is not included. What IS included is federal privilege, measured by the revenue which its exercise produces. That privilege takes the form of essentially three things: Federal government employment; the performance of the functions of a federal public office; and being engaged in a federally licensed business.

As the Supreme Court instructs us in Brushaber versus Union Pacific R.R. (and many other cases) taxation on income is *"...in its nature an excise..."*

In Flint versus Stone Tracy the court tells us that the requirement to pay excise taxes *"...involves the exercise of privilege."*

The Second Circuit Court of Appeals puts it succinctly in American Airways versus Wallace: *"The terms "excise tax" and "privilege tax" are synonymous. The two are often used interchangeably."*

F. Morse Hubbard, a Congressional legislative draftsman, explained this in testimony before Congress in 1943, saying:

> *"The income tax is, therefore, not a tax on income as such. It is an excise tax with respect to certain activities and privileges which is measured by reference to the income which they produce. The income is not the subject of the tax: it is the basis for determining the amount of tax"*

I'm confident that the 16th amendment has popped into many heads over the last few seconds, as the standard IRS-type explanation if presented with the Constitutional prohibition on unapportioned direct taxes is to suggest that the 16th amendment did away with the apportionment requirement. This is simply not true.

Almost immediately after the passage of the 16th amendment, a test case went to the Supreme Court, brought by a New Yorker named Frank Brushaber. He was attempting to stop the application of the income tax to dividends to be paid against his railroad company stock, and argued that the tax amounted to a direct tax without apportionment, and was therefore unconstitutional, the 16th amendment notwithstanding-- in fact, he argued in part that the amendment itself was unconstitutional. The court corrected him, saying,

> *"We are of opinion, however, that the confusion is not inherent, but rather arises from the conclusion that the 16th Amendment provides for a hitherto unknown power of taxation; that is, a power to levy an income tax which, although direct, should not be subject to the regulation of apportionment applicable to all other direct taxes. And the far-reaching effect of this erroneous assumption will be made clear by generalizing the many contentions advanced in argument to support it..."*

The court proceeds to discuss these many contentions, leading it eventually point out that,

> *"...it clearly results that the proposition and the contentions under it, if acceded to, would cause one provision of the Constitution to destroy another; that is, they would result in bringing the provisions of the Amendment exempting a direct tax from apportionment into irreconcilable conflict with the general requirement that all direct taxes be apportioned."*

Confused? Here is the key: The 16th amendment does not say anything about a *direct* tax without apportionment-- it merely provides for a tax on *income* without apportionment, and "income" does not mean "all that comes in", or, as Smith put it, *"every different species of revenue"*. What it means is the benefit of federal privilege, as discussed a few moments ago. Indeed, during the course of its ruling in the Brushaber case, the Supreme Court goes so far as to point out that should the term "income" come-- through craft or sloppy usage-- to be treated as "all that comes in" in relation to a tax, the apportionment rule would have to be applied, even though the name of what was being taxed had not changed.

The fact is, the term "income" had long been used statutorily by the time of the 16th amendment. The first income tax act had been passed in 1862, and was followed by many others. The meaning of the term was fixed and consistent throughout those enactments, and those taxes had been upheld by the courts during that time, because a tax on federal privilege, the exercise of which is a wholly optional and voluntary activity, is an indirect tax, to which the apportionment rule never applied.

The 16th amendment came about not because it was necessary to implement a tax on "income", but because in an 1894 case, Pollock versus Farmer's Loan and Trust, the Supreme Court had said that even the benefit of federal privilege could not be taxed if receiving it was connected with the ownership of private property. This was another railroad stock-related case (railroads having been declared by the Supreme Court in the very early 1890's to be federal instrumentalities, making revenue associated with them "income").

The plaintiff, Pollock, objected to the imposition of the tax nonetheless, arguing that because the revenue by which the tax was to be measured proceeded from his private property-- that is to say, the stock he owned-- to tax that revenue was to tax the private property itself, and thus such a tax would be direct, and must be apportioned. The Supreme Court agreed, and the country proceeded in due course to propose and more-or-less ratify the 16th amendment, giving Congress the power to lay a tax on incomes, from whatever source derived, without regard to any census or enumeration. Nothing changed about the meaning of the term "income"-- the amendment simply provided that resort to the private property source of the income could no longer be used to frustrate the tax. "Income" remains what it always has been-- federal privilege, measured by the dollars it produces.

All of this is directly and unambiguously reflected in the statutory structure of the tax as written. The word "wages" for instance, as used in federal revenue law is not a word, it is a custom-defined legal term, meaning "the remuneration paid to federal officers and employees". Similarly, the phrase "trade or business" in the revenue law is defined as "the performance of the functions of a public office". "Employee", "employer" and "employment" are all custom-defined terms in the law.

Like the term "income" when used in relation to federal tax law, none of these legal <u>terms</u> have the common meanings of the otherwise identical <u>words</u> that we use in everyday language. There is, however, an elaborate and mature scheme in place by which those who are NOT federal officers and employees, and who are NOT engaged in the performance of the functions of a public office, are made to appear in the eyes of the law as though they were those beneficiaries of federal privilege, and are therefore taxable on their receipts.

This scheme involves the routine creation of evidence by Americans who make payments to their fellows in which such payments are declared to be the payment of "wages" *as defined in the revenue law*, or to have been made in the course of the payers or recipients "trade or business" *as that phrase is defined in the revenue law.* One or the other of these two declarations lies behind every W-2 or 1099 issued by anyone and about anyone.

Who among the business owners here has ever actually read the law under which a W-2 is created and submitted? Any who had would have found that, by statute, what is to be listed on a W-2 is not simply 'wages'-- it is *only* and *explicitly* to be *"wages as defined in sections 3401 and 3121 of the Internal Revenue Code"*.

Which of you, in submitting a 1099 to some poor contractor, with a copy being put on record with the IRS, has taken the time to notice that the instructions for filling out the form explicitly and clearly say it is only to be used to list payments made in the course of a "trade or business", and even if having noticed this, has followed up and discovered what "trade or business" means in the revenue law? Well, you're not alone. Every year millions of such documents are produced about millions of Americans, and it is on the basis of those "information returns" as they are known, that a tax liability is presumed to exist for those about whom they are created. There are a few more involved subtleties to the structure of the scheme, of course, but that is the heart of it.

Obviously, everyone with respect for the rule of law-- both Constitutional, and subordinate statutory law-- should stop creating false evidence, if they have been doing so. Furthermore, those about whom false evidence has been created should rebut and correct it. Our legal system, being an adversarial system in which claims are sorted out based upon competing evidence, provides for such rebuttals and contests institutionally, and nowhere more so than in the tax system. In fact, the IRS itself produces forms intended for just that purpose.

This is not to say that the "service" encourages such corrections, of course, even when made on their own forms. In fact, it will resist explaining that you can make them; and it will resist acknowledging or abiding by them once made with all the warmth, charm, and helpful demeanor of a rabid junk-yard dog with a toothache. Because the simple fact is, once erroneous evidence about "income" received has been challenged, the government's established claim to an associated tax correspondingly evaporates.

However, what YOU attest to is your business, not theirs, and challenging what others say about you is your right as well. We have no bureaucratic kings in America empowered to say only one side's testimony is worthy of consideration, or to declare one's to be true and another's not.

The Founders provided a prudent tax structure for America. Under that structure, direct, unavoidable taxes require a straightforward declaration of purpose and amount-- and accountable representative endorsement-- as each such tax is a one-time affair, and is collected by the state governments from their own citizens, thus keeping the mechanisms closer to the people. All other lawful federal taxes, being indirect, share the characteristic of optional, voluntary citizen participation and the requirement that their overall burden be uniformly distributed throughout the union, while possibly being perpetual once enacted.

With any other audience, I would be tempted to proceed with a discussion of why insisting on strict adherence to this Constitutional structure is so important, but I suspect that with you this is not necessary. I am confident that everyone here is fully conscious of the ills attendant upon what has become an institutional disregard of that structure, effectively resulting in perpetual, involuntary and unaccountable taxation which diverts a river of wealth-- and consequently power-- out of the hands of the citizenry and into the control of the state. We all know that once so diverted, that wealth is used to corruptly secure incumbencies, to pay off favored special interests at the expense of the disfavored, to inordinately swell the influence of the federal government over our state and local institutions, and to justify and finance the swarms of officers sent forth every day to harass us and eat out our substance.

America cannot long endure a steady assault upon her intended design by this process and the mechanisms and subterfuges necessary for its sustenance. I hope that you'll all join me in striving to put an end to it.

Thank you.

Update:

The United States Supreme Court, in a despicable 6-3 ruling in Ashcroft v. Raich (re-titled Gonzales v. Raich), demonstrated its willingness to utterly defy logic-- and disregard the clearly-stated intent of the Framers-- in service to the boundless ambitions of Congress. Thus, I am proposing the following amendment to the United States Constitution:

"The power of Congress to regulate Commerce with foreign Nations, and among the several States, and with the Indian tribes shall be exercised solely for the purpose and to the effect of ensuring that such commerce is unhindered and unburdened, other than by such tariffs on foreign imports as are elsewhere provided for herein."

This amendment actually just spells out the Framer's intent in creating the commerce clause in the first place, but it has become obvious that this sort of emphasis is necessary. I would be grateful for your help in seeing this amendment adopted-- which will involve initiating and promoting action in the legislatures of the several States (and at the grass-roots level), if it is to be effective.

Upholding the Law
෨෬൩෬ൾ

There's a wonderful old fable called "The Emperor's New Clothes", in which a pair of scoundrels con money from a foolish sovereign by claiming the ability to spin clothes from pure gold. The Emperor, eager to possess what he should have known was impossible, gives the conmen his gold and a room in which to work, but prudently endeavors to supervise them through the eyes of various members of his court, whom he dispatches at intervals to observe and report on the progress of the work. However, the two conmen, though actually engaging in nothing but pantomime, deploy sheer audacity and a subtle exploitation of the human psychology to successfully oblige each such officer to conclude that the imaginary clothes which the pair claim to be sewing are visible to everyone but himself.

The scheme is masterfully cunning. Expansive and eloquent descriptions of the non-existent work are presented to each courtier arriving to conduct an inspection. At the same time, each is informed of an especially marvelous property of the cloth: It is possessed of such subtle perfection that it is invisible to all but the most capable and competent! Thus each inspector is discouraged from believing the evidence of his own eyes, or at least from voicing any doubts about the conmen's work.

Quite the contrary, in fact. Each victim of the scam is seduced into personal participation in its furtherance-- vociferously parroting the conmen in description and praise of the magnificence of the cloth, and thereby supporting the pressure on his fellows to do the same. The cunning process instantly created a community of interest in the perpetuation-- even the elaboration-- of the illusion.

So, the fantasy is spun and thrives, not only unchallenged but ever-fed, until the Emperor himself, having been told over and over by all of his subordinates what wonderful work the conmen are doing (and, no less than any other, unwilling to raise doubts regarding his own fitness for office), effusively praises the invisible garments with which he is at last fitted. Chilly, but entirely taken in, the naked sovereign marches into the public square to show off his new finery. There, the townspeople, also aware of the "special properties" of the cloth, ooh and ah.

Like the courtiers before them, the commoners carefully suppress themselves, and declaim to each other as to the magnificence of the Emperor's new clothes, until at last a young child, unencumbered by pride, speaks the plain truth revealed to his own eyes and announces that the Emperor has no clothes! The spell is broken, and everyone awakens, but the thieves have snuck away with the gold, which they have, of course, simply been pocketing all the while.

I hope that everyone shares this most educational tale with their children. This fable offer much insight into human behavior in general, and the behavior of placeholders in a hierarchy (as opposed to free-agents in a meritocracy) in particular. More importantly, this clever allegory can help us understand the simple mechanics of one of the key processes by which the rule of law is being corrupted in America today, and what it is that each of us is called upon to do in order that the law may be restored and upheld.

What Do We Mean By 'Rule Of Law'?

The phrase 'rule of law' is commonly understood to mean that once the law has been written, it is the final word, for practical purposes. No edict issuing forth from any tyrant can override it, nor can any man escape its authority, regardless of position or place. This understanding is sound enough, as far as it goes.

However, a more fundamental aspect of the 'rule of law' concept is that in order for 'the law' to rule, the laws must be made *according to the rules.* That is, they must remain within the limits of the legitimate authority of the lawmaker; they must be made effectively and meaningfully known to those to whom they apply, and they must be clear in their command. Any "law" which fails in any of these respects is, at best, more a burden on the polity than a benefit; at worst, it is a tool of despotism of one variety or another.

For instance, it is obvious that a "law" which is a mere declaration of the tyrant is no true law. Nor is the unrestrained whim of the mob. In the former case, the necessary delegation of authority from the polity is lacking, at the least. In the latter case, typically, authority beyond that which CAN be delegated is exercised.

Regarding sufficiency of notice, the evils and illegitimacy of a "law" which bides in secrecy until deployed against an unwitting target seem almost too obvious to even allude to. However, such "laws" were well-enough known to America's founding fathers that they felt obliged to include a prohibition in the federal Constitution against one version-- "ex-post facto" laws, that is, new "laws" which take cognizance of previously engaged-in behavior. Furthermore, while not quite stepping across the line into outright disregard of the "no secret law" rule yet, the establishment of secret courts such as the Foreign Intelligence Surveillance Act court, the implementation of unpublished policies such as those regarding the furnishing of identification before flying in a commercial aircraft, and the several "retroactive" tax increases which have occurred in recent years reveal a systemic disdain on the part of the current state toward this simple, common-sense rule.

This disdain is most dangerously expressed in claims of extra-Constitutional executive authority in time of crisis, which is nothing more and nothing less than an effort at justifying the administration of secret law. "Law" which is not deliberated nor published, but merely springs forth from the mind of an executive on the fly couldn't be more secret (nor less legitimate).

Beyond legitimacy of authority and sufficiency of notice, the chief rule in the 'rules of law' is "clarity of command". It is here that we can be instructed by the wisdom in the fable of the Emperor's New Clothes.

The law must say what it means, and mean what it says. Without clarity a 'law' is nothing more than a weapon in the hands of whoever is allowed to declare its meaning-- an invisible thing, the effects and consequences of which are only revealed to us as we are made the targets of its application. In no way is such a "law" the property or product of the people in whose name it is theoretically administered. The sense of this can be concisely apprehended by considering Josef Stalin's wise observation that,

> *"He who votes decides nothing; he who counts the votes decides everything."*

Of precisely the same character is the reality that,

> *"He who makes the law exercises no power, if he who enforces the law gets to decide what the law means."*

The fortunate reality is that American law IS clear-- it DOES say what it means and it DOES mean what it says. Nonetheless, the American legal system IS used as a weapon (and a gravy-train) by scoundrels who have conned their way into the position of declaring the meaning of the law to the rest of us. These scoundrels have seduced and intimidated the rest of us into entertaining the fantasy that, rather than the plain and sturdy homespun that it really is, our law now has magical properties, too complicated and subtle to be understood by commoners. We have been conned into nodding our heads, and letting ourselves be told all about this amazing law-- how it works, and how it can be exercised-- even when the tale keeps changing in a way that is always to the benefit of the conmen, and always to the diminishment of ourselves. But this amazing pretense is just a cheap fraud, capitalizing on our all-too-widespread ignorance of the essential character of true law.

True law, legitimate law, is the law of the people-- it is not the product nor the province of special knowledge, or a privileged class, and it cannot be. It is the essence of true law that it be of the people's making, and for the people's purpose, and that it be accessible by the people and comprehensible to the people-- therefore simple, straightforward, explicit and limited. Axiomatically, a law such that the legal duty which it mandates, and the limits of that legal duty, are not fully clear to the average citizen is illegitimate and void, regardless of the forms or persons by which it may have been crafted or interpreted. As the United States Supreme Court points out in Connally v. General Const. Co., 269 U.S. 385 (1926):

> "...a statute which either forbids or requires the doing of an act in terms so vague that men of common intelligence must necessarily guess at its meaning and differ as to its application violates the first essential of due process of law."

It is self-evident that any law which is not clearly comprehensible to at least a majority of the people is not, in any meaningful way, of the people's making. In fact, such a law *cannot* be of the people's making, for how can it be said that someone has made something that they themselves do not understand?

Nor can such a "law" be legitimately administered for any purpose, for how can anyone be held to account for the violation of an incomprehensible requirement? It is no answer to these simple realities that 'interpreters' of the law are available. To rest there is to accept the establishment of an aristocracy, contrary to natural law as well as to the Constitution. Further, "interpreted law" is inevitably a fluid and amorphous thing. Such "law" changes with each individual scrying. It is ever and always in doubt; and it is inherently unequal in its application-- either for the benefit, or to the dismay, of any given object of its attention. "Interpreted law" is inherently secret law by nature. True law must be visible to the eyes of the people.

*****

True law delivers justice through equality of access, a scrupulous regard for clarity and a scrupulous respect for rights. It embraces only such principles and purposes which can each be upheld without a violation or compromise of any other, and which can be contemplated, without art or artifice, by all to whom it applies. While these characteristics necessarily leave much outside its reach, it is only thus that the law can meet the prime requirement of legitimacy.

Unfortunately, many years ago, America let itself be distracted from the simple principles of true law by a grand fantasy of law that is all things to all people, which regulates and rectifies every imagined imperfection of life, and fulfills every desire. We became dazzled by enticing visions of a utopian perfection of outcome spun by scoundrels who only asked that the law be put into their hands for spinning.

Like the Emperor in the fable, each American unwisely delegated the responsibility for overseeing their treasure to others. These others, wittingly or unwittingly, merely repeated the lies, finding that to be the safest or easiest course, or knowing no better than anyone else. Thus, we all became victims of the trap. Like the Emperor, we walk through our country naked, cold and insecure, stripped of the benefits of true law, and we do so without protest. As those in the fable were about the Emperor's new clothes, so have we Americans become about our law. Each of us concludes that while he or she perceives the law as incomprehensible, illegitimate, and flawed, everyone else apparently does not. The problem, each of us individually imagine, must be with ourselves.

Individually, we all know that whether a business does or does not meet OSHA standards in its facilities and practices has no affect on "commerce between the several states", as would be alleged in a prosecution for failing to do so. Individually, we all know that dictating the disposition of a wetland area on private property to serve an alleged collective interest in its preservation is a taking of private property for public use. Individually, we all know that a Constitutional amendment was needed to authorize federal prohibition of alcohol and a Constitutional amendment is needed to authorize a legitimate federal prohibition of marijuana. Individually, we all know that a seizure of property without a trial, whether called a "civil forfeiture", or by any other name, is a violation of due process.

Individually, we all know that the United States Constitution is shorter and simpler than the instructions for assembling a bicycle. Individually, we all know that the nine great legal minds sitting on the Supreme Court, and all those lesser lights sitting on all the lesser courts, and the swarms of government attorneys practicing before them for lo, these past two hundred and fifteen years have not been struggling, in their tortured interpretations-- and subsequent interpretations of previous interpretations-- to figure it out, so as to scrupulously abide by its restrictions. Individually, we all know that instead, these specialists have been struggling to devolve it into a "living law" by virtue of which they are elevated to a legal priesthood.

Individually, we all know that the growth of State power over our lives, which is both a market-broadening interest of its symbiotic beneficiaries, and the inevitable consequence of make-it-up-as-you-go-along jurisprudence, is rapidly erecting the infrastructure of totalitarianism, conditioning an ever-more poorly educated population to the habits of subordination to government, and strengthening the general perception of the law as fundamentally outside the ken of the average citizen in the corrupt cycle that is the essence of the con.

Despite all of us knowing all these truths, every day millions of citizens are constrained in their dignity and liberty by fear of prosecution or suit over their management of their own business affairs, and other private decisions-- or indeed suffer loss in such prosecutions or suits. Every day, thousands of citizens are constrained in their dignity and liberty by fear of prosecution or suit in the disposition of their own land-- or indeed suffer loss in such prosecutions or suits. Every year, thousands of citizens lose, in the aggregate, billions of dollars worth of property to seizures without trial; and every year virtually every adult citizen is bullied and intimidated into declaring themselves lawfully taxable by a code that neither they, their attorney, their CPA or the IRS thugs shaking them down have ever read.

Every day a million offenses of government lawlessness are visited upon us and our neighbors because, like the Emperor's court, we are each persuaded by the conmen to believe-- or behave as though we believe-- an obvious and corrupt lie. So we meekly do what we're told. We sign where we're told, parrot what we're told, think what we're told, denounce our neighbor when we're told, indict our neighbor when we're told, arrest our neighbor when we're told, convict our neighbor when we're told, and haul away our neighbor's property when we're told. Every day, dazzled by fine words and fanciful images, and cowed into silence by fear of looking foolish, we sacrifice a bit more at the direction of the priesthood of the "living law". Every day, the fabric of our true law becomes more threadbare.

In the fable, the conmen stole the money and left town, content to enrich themselves and move on. In America today, the conmen have moved right in, for they've learned that their little scheme serves the interests of powerful factions, and have become partners in a cozy little relationship. Political demagogues, collectivists, bureaucratic tyrants, and other buyers and sellers of power over individual citizens are steady customers for the legal theocrats, trading protection and feeding-rights for usefully creative deconstructions of the law. It's the oldest game in the book, in fact-- one played by kings and priests since time immemorial.

So, What Do We Do?

First, we open our eyes, and, like the little boy in the Emperor's New Clothes, recognize and admit some disquieting truths. Among them is that restoring the rule of law-- the true law-- is going to be resisted by the entrenched beneficiaries of the prevailing status quo, and is thus going to require dedication and sacrifice. It is not going to be accomplished by a part-time effort.

John Adams, speaking during the time of the American revolution, instructs us thusly:

> "*I must study politics and war that my sons may have liberty to study mathematics and philosophy. My sons ought to study mathematics and philosophy, geography, natural history, naval architecture, navigation, commerce and agriculture in order to give their children a right to study painting, poetry, music, architecture, statuary, tapestry, and porcelain.*"

Adams' formula worked out, as far as it went. But he stopped short in his prediction-- incapable of imagining, from the perspective of his own immersion in affairs of substance and moment, what would actually come to pass in the fullness of time. Had he looked further, he would have reluctantly continued, "*...so that my more distant descendants have the leisure to study television, and the sports page.*"

We cannot afford such distractions. We must turn off the tube and tune in to reality.

We must study politics, and war.

*****

Edmund Burke, a British Member of Parliament and contemporary of Adams, addressed parliament in 1775 regarding the aspirations of the colonists for liberty, observing that,

> "*In this character of the Americans, a love of freedom is the predominating feature which marks and distinguishes the whole: and as an ardent is always a jealous affection, your colonies become suspicious, restive, and untractable, whenever they see the least attempt to wrest from them by force, or shuffle from them by chicane, what they think the only advantage worth living for.*"

Burke goes on to further describe aspects of the American character, and the reasons why Britain cannot succeed in maintaining the subjugation of the colonies. His last argument (prior to dryly pointing out that three thousand miles of ocean hinder the British purpose) is this:

> *"Permit me, Sir, to add another circumstance in our colonies, which contributes no mean part towards the growth and effect of this untractable spirit. I mean their education. In no country perhaps in the world is the law so general a study. The profession itself is numerous and powerful; and in most provinces it takes the lead. The greater number of the deputies sent to the congress were lawyers. But all who read, and most do read, endeavour to obtain some smattering in that science. I have been told by an eminent bookseller, that in no branch of his business, after tracts of popular devotion, were so many books as those on the law exported to the plantations. The colonists have now fallen into the way of printing them for their own use."*

Burke correctly recognized that it was the American's knowledge of the law that made them a people impossible to hold under illegitimate power. Not because that study reveals a magic spell that makes tyrants and would-be tyrants dry up and blow away, but because a study of the law arms the student with the moral certainty needed to sustain the long-term commitment which the struggle for liberty against the ambitions of despotism always requires.

We must study the law, and arm ourselves with the moral certainty that the defense of liberty requires.

*****

Thomas Jefferson observed that,
"It is the natural course of things that government should gain ground and liberty yield."

In saying this, Jefferson did not mean that the defense of liberty is a fool's game. He meant that like rust-- its counterpart in the physical world-- political corruption never sleeps, but those against whom it contends, do.

Those sons and grandsons of John Adams, who set aside the study of the arts of politics and war, turn their attention instead to other pursuits once the battle for liberty seems well-fought, and won. They install their servants into positions of responsibility and immerse themselves in their families, their businesses, and their pleasures. They lose the habit of jealously guarding their rights.

They become complacent, and distracted, and when the servants offer to take charge of certain of their affairs, those distracted and complacent sons and grandsons are compliant. It is then not long before those distracted and complacent sons and grandsons return home to find that the locks on the house have changed, and the helpful servants hold the keys.

The fact is, the battle for liberty is never over. Power WILL be exercised over everything that it can be in this world. Who exercises it is determined not as a matter of right-- which can be sorted out, and written down, and considered finished. Who exercises power is determined as a matter of will. Frederick Douglass explained this to us when he thundered,

> *"Power concedes nothing without a demand. It never did and it never will. Find out just what any people will quietly submit to and you have the exact measure of the injustice and wrong which will be imposed on them, and these will continue till they have been resisted with either words or blows, or with both. The limits of*

> *tyrants are prescribed by the endurance of those whom they suppress."*

Rust never sleeps, and neither can we. We must put aside our distractions; abandon our complacency; and study the law, and the arts of politics and war.

*****

If You Perceive That Your Government Is Doing Wrong And You Do Nothing, It May Well Be That Your Government Is Corrupt, But It Is A Certainty That You Are

The mechanism of the con in the Emperor's New Clothes was the substitution of the thief's pretense for the self-evident truth available to the eyes of everyone else involved, by means of simple but effective psychology. The scoundrels used the fear of being out of step with the crowd to intimidate each and every member of that crowd-- all of whom saw exactly the same thing, and harbored exactly the same truth-- into silence. They lured, and seduced, and slyly threatened each of their victims into self-suppression. The scoundrels made monkeys out of everyone else involved-- monkeys who saw no evil, heard no evil, and spoke no evil, long enough for the thieves to creep away with all the monkey's treasure.

Today, here in America, you and I are encouraged to play the part of dumb animals, cowed into the denial of the evidence of our own eyes. We are urged to join in, and be a part of the corruption ourselves, by standing silent as the conmen steal our gold.

Don't do it.

Raise Your Voice.

Speak Your Truth.

Never Abandon The Field Of Battle.

Uphold The Law.

ℰᎧᏟᏸᎧᏟᏒ

Pete Hendrickson makes his home in Commerce Township, Michigan, with his wife Doreen, daughter Kathryn Elizabeth, son Thomas Jefferson, and far too many furred, feathered and finned companions to identify by name.